P9-CRQ-754

PastorPower

Martha Ellen Stortz

Abingdon Press / Nashville

PastorPower

Copyright © 1993 by Abingdon Press

All rights reserved.
No part of this work may be reproduced or transmitted in any form or by any means, electronic or mechanical, including photocopying and recording, or by any information storage or retrieval system, except as may be expressly permitted by the 1976 Copyright Act or in writing from the publisher. Requests for permission should be addressed to Abingdon Press, 201 Eighth Avenue South, Nashville TN 37203.

This book is printed on acid-free, recycled paper.

Library of Congress Cataloging-in-Publication Data

Stortz, Martha Ellen, 1952–
    Pastorpower/Martha Ellen Stortz.
        p. cm.
    Includes index.
    ISBN 0-687-08671-X (alk. paper)
        1. Clergy—Office. 2. Power (Christian theology). 3. Pastoral theology. I. Title.
BV660.2.S78 1993
253—dc20   92-46305
                                                                                                              CIP

Scripture quotations, except for brief paraphrases or unless otherwise noted, are from the New Revised Standard Version Bible, Copyright 1989 by the Division of Christian Education of the National Council of the Churches of Christ in the USA. Used by permission.

"Giants, Wizards, and Dwarfs" (pp. 13-14) is from *All I Really Need to Know I Learned in Kindergarten* by Robert Fulghum. Copyright © 1986, 1988 by Robert Fulghum. Reprinted by permission of Villard Books, a division of Random House, Inc.

93 94 95 96 97 98 99 00 01 02   —   10 9 8 7 6 5 4 3 2 1

MANUFACTURED IN THE UNITED STATES OF AMERICA

for my father
William Clifford Stortz
(1916–1992)

89001

Contents

Contents

Preface

Pondering Questions of Power or Where Can I Get a Cup of Coffee at This Hour?

Dave's 24-Hour Coffee Shop is on Broadway and 42nd Street in Oakland, where lower Rockridge, a gentrified neighborhood that stretches into the Oakland hills, meets the more serious urban landscape of the city of Oakland. It's difficult to locate Dave's: Is it in Rockridge or the city serious?

It's difficult to place Dave's in a specific decade. The large, blinking, 24-hour day-or-night neon outside spells "coffee shop," but Dave's is a dinosaur of a diner from an era before coffee shops had discovered the New World. Dave's decor is an orange that paint stores no longer carry, with linoleum floors and lots of chrome. You seat yourself, and you can sit either at the counter on a swivel-seated stool or in one of the orange booths. Every place setting has a coffee cup and saucer; the cup is always inverted. Before you've had a chance to look at the menu, a waitress appears, turns over the cup, fills it full of coffee. If you ask for decaf, she frowns in incomprehension. The waitresses look like they've been imported from the 1950s: They all seem to have horn-rimmed glasses and beehives. When you finally get a chance to look at the menu, you find that you can order breakfast all day.

Dave's clientele is even more difficult to locate. Everyone has come from somewhere else. There's a racial mix: African American, Asian American, Native American, Caucasian American, and students from the California College of the Arts and Crafts, who defy classification entirely. There's an economic mix at Dave's as well. Street people, who've panhandled enough coin for the Breakfast Special, sit in booths next to Rockridge professionals, who've escaped cellular phones and fax machines for an ambience that ignores them. There are even a few tourists from Berkeley, who refuse to believe that coffee can be made without an espresso machine.

Dave's is in all ways difficult to place, which is probably why my colleague Richard and I decided to meet there. We'd been working together leading a class at the seminary called "integrative growth group." It's a required part of the curriculum for the professional ministry track, but it abandons the standard academic regimen of required papers and texts and focuses instead on the important but amorphous task of integrating the work of academic study, field work, spiritual development, and sense of vocation. Each faculty teams with a parish pastor in the leadership of these groups. For three years I, a white, female layperson and seminary professor was teamed with Richard, a black, male clergyperson with a parish on the Oakland-Berkeley border. We were assigned eight first-year students and a room on campus and given an hour and a half each week to focus on the task of integration.

What Richard and I figured out during the course of the semester over Dave's cut-with-a-knife coffee was that we were each extremely reluctant to exercise any kind of leadership in the group, particularly in the presence of the other. As a woman and an African American, we had each experienced power largely as domination and oppression. Now that we each had power, we were loathe to replicate those past histories for the students in our group, but absolutely clueless about any alternatives. Moreover, I was anxious about exercising my authority in the group, because I was afraid it might be and might be perceived as racist and professorial. Richard was reluctant to exercise his authority in the group, because he was afraid it might be and might be perceived as sexist and clericalist. Besides, neither one of us really believed an institution would give a black pastor and a white laywoman charge over anything. We were both just waiting for the other shoe to drop.

It's so difficult to locate anything at Dave's, that no one even blinked when a white woman and a black man in a clerical collar wandered in from somewhere else and got lost in conversation for several hours. But after several sessions, Richard and I were able to articulate and even to address some of these various and nefarious dynamics. This book is in part the issue of those conversations.

In keeping with the spirit of Dave's, this book does not attempt to locate anyone. That is to say, that if the reader uses the book as a map, she will surely get lost. The best way to walk into the book is the way one would walk into Dave's: expect some disjunctions in time and place and head for an empty stool at the counter. Don't decide anything until that first cup of coffee, and if you still can't decide anything, order the Breakfast Special. It's always good, and it "seconds the real world."[1]

Probably this is a book for those who love to eat, rather than those who love to cook. Those who love to cook may be tempted to use it as a recipe book, adding the proper amount of humor, generosity, and truth-telling to concoct a desirable leadership style. I issue a caution at the outset: These observations are not intended to be so directive. Take a cue from those who love to eat and linger over each chapter, savoring the various ingredients. The book will help you identify them: here a bit of ginger, shallots, chopped carrots, and—that must be lemon juice! The book may help you rearrange them for the taste of your own palate: You would use lime juice instead. But, if the book edifies, it is because of the mixture of ingredients. No one, after all, would want to sit down to a plateful of fresh grated ginger. If the book satisfies, it is because of the adjustments you made for your own discrete taste. (But I come from a school of cooking as mnemonic alchemy. We are untutored by cookbooks, but have good palatal recall and are always eager to reproduce good meals from a distinctly remembered past.) For those who love to eat, the delight is not in the analysis, but in the taste. Finally, those who love to eat never worry about where they are—they are lost in the most unlikely places! They are more interested in what they are eating.

This book examines three kinds of leadership: "power over," which can be seen as sovereign, parental, or bureaucratic power; "power within" or charismatic power; and "power with" or coactive power. The discussion of each form of power is presented in a case study, and the case study both critiques and illustrates the analysis of the kind of power in question. Finally, these models of leadership are analyzed theologically, from an emerging trinitarian perspective, to see how theological understandings of power might form, inform, and transform the use of power described.

The first two case studies are presented as they were told to me: in first-person singular. I did not try to verify, qualify, or refute the information I received. Indeed, part of the burden of analysis is understanding the speaker: on whose behalf is he speaking? whom does she represent? where is he standing? The third case study is presented in third-person: the perspective of the omniscient author, a perspective which, by that point, ought to be by definition problematic. No author is omniscient, and no author free of assumptions.

My assumptions are legion. Those most conscious and most crucial to me are the following:

1. I adopt Michel Foucault's understanding of power as something that "circulates" and that people and institutions simultaneously both exercise and are affected by.[2] I am concerned to examine three ways in which power circulates in churches, with attention to its effects.

2. I adopt a typology of power—"power over," "power within," and "power with"—which itself seems to be in popular circulation. Yet, I am concerned with the equally popular tendency to dismiss all discussion of "power over," as oppressive and dominative, and to elevate uncritically "power within" and "power with" as alternatives.[3] I want to look at the kinds and conditions under which "power over" may be appropriately exercised, as well as the problems inherent in exercise of both "power with" and "power within."

3. I assume a critical appropriation of feminist theory. An initial assumption among feminists that all discussion of power was patriarchal has dissipated, and provocative work currently being done on power by feminist authors of various disciplines has been most formative in this work.[4]

4. I assume that theological dimensions of power have the ability to form, inform, and transform its exercise. Thus, I investigate a trinitarian articulation of divine power and its implications for leadership.

The meal has been a long time in preparation. Specific colleagues and consultants have helped in the making and preparation of this book. I would like especially to thank the students in my "Power and Ministry" seminars at the Graduate Theological Union, whose insights, questions, and challenges have both extended the time of preparation and made the fare richer. My colleagues at Pacific Lutheran Theological Seminary and in the Graduate Theological Union have encouraged and critiqued various stages of the preparation. From the seminary, I would like to thank especially Dr. Gary Pence, whose leadership development project originally paired my colleague Richard and I and provided a forum in which we could discuss our experience. The Reverend Donna Duensing shared with me her pastoral heart and insight. We also laughed a lot. Finally, Dean Timothy Lull, when he was not able to relieve me of institutional duties, offered dynamic commiseration. From the Graduate Theological Union, I would like to thank the women faculty in general, whose comments on an early section of the manuscript sharpened the argument considerably. In particular, I must thank Dr. Clare B. Fischer at the Thomas Starr King School of Ministry for her continuing friendship, her collegiality, and her appetite for conversation. The Reverend Mary Hardy and Clayton Crawley assisted in the final fragile stages of preparation, insisting that the manuscript be linked to the concrete experience of ministry. Author and anthropologist João Guilherme Biehl read and critiqued the final draft of this manuscript. Joanne Burrows attended to details and the index with grace, efficiency, and humor. Dr. Paul Franklyn at Abingdon Press well deserves the title of midwife to the whole process of preparation. Finally, I thank the Reverend Richard Wallace, now at the Lutheran House of Studies in Atlanta, and Dave, whoever he is, at the 24-hour coffee shop.

For the friends, family, and colleagues herein named—and not!—I am thankful. My work and my life are more gracious for their presences, their absences, their always surprising abilities to see what I cannot.

Enjoy—and adjust the spices to taste.

Introduction

A Parable of Power

Giants, Wizards, and Dwarfs was the game to play.

Being left in charge of about eighty children seven to ten years old, while their parents were off doing parenty things, I mustered my troops in the church social hall and explained the game. It's a large-scale version of Rock, Paper, and Scissors, and involves some intellectual decision making. But the real purpose of the game is to make a lot of noise and run around chasing people until nobody knows which side you are on or who won.

Organizing a roomful of wired-up gradeschoolers into two teams, explaining the rudiments of the game, achieving consensus on group identity—all this is no mean accomplishment, but we did it with a right good will and were ready to go.

The excitement of the chase had reached a critical mass. I yelled out: "You have to decide *now* which you are—a GIANT, a WIZARD, or a DWARF!"

While the groups huddled in frenzied, whispered consultation, a tug came at my pants leg. A small child stands there looking up, and asks in a small, concerned voice, "Where do the Mermaids stand?"

Where do the Mermaids stand?

A long pause. A *very* long pause. "Where do the Mermaids stand?" says I.

"Yes. You see, I am a Mermaid."

"There are no such things as Mermaids."

"Oh, yes, I am one!"

She did not relate to being a Giant, a Wizard, or a Dwarf. She knew her category. Mermaid. And was not about to leave the game and go over and stand against the wall where a loser would stand. She intended to participate, wherever Mermaids fit into the scheme of things. Without giving up dignity or identity. She took it for granted that there was a place for Mermaids and that I would know just where.

Well, where DO the Mermaids stand? All the "Mermaids"—all those who are different, who do not fit the norm and who do not accept the available boxes and pigeonholes?

Answer that question and you can build a school, a nation, or a world on it.

What was my answer at the moment? Every once in a while I say the right thing. "The Mermaid stands right here by the King of the Sea!" says I. (*Yes, right here by the King's Fool, I thought to myself.*) So we stood there hand in hand, reviewing the troops of Wizards and Giants and Dwarfs as they roiled by in wild disarray.

It is not true, by the way, that mermaids do not exist. I know at least one personally. I have held her hand.[1]

A reader can always only guess at an author's intent, and that guess is itself affected by the reader's own secret thoughts and desires. I will try to be explicit about mine here.

On Parables

Whatever Robert Fulghum's intent, I propose that we treat the story as a parable, more specifically, as a parable about power. Treating the story as a parable suggests that it cannot be locked into a single meaning or reduced to a simple moral.[2] To enter the world of a parable is to enter the world of multiple meanings.

Preachers have preached for centuries on the finite number of parables contained in the four Gospels, always discovering something new. These tough little stories puzzled audiences then as now. Indeed, puzzlement was the teller's intent. Initially, the disciples begged for interpretation, but interpretations proved even more baffling than the stories themselves. The Twelve realized that they would have to settle for ambiguity. Apparently, the truths of the Kingdom were multiple and could be seen from many different perspectives simultaneously. Perhaps part of Jesus' message was in the medium in which he spoke most frequently: these verbal knots named parables.

In an effort to manage the multiplicity of meanings, biblical editors have tried to narrow their scope. Their slogans are embedded in italicized headings at the tops of columns of the Bible's prose; these have passed into common ecclesial parlance. We speak about "the parable of the prodigal son"—not "the parable of the gracious father." We preach on "the parable of the lost coin"—not "the parable of the found coin" or "the parable of the woman finding." We study "the parable of the Samaritan woman"—not "the parable of the forgotten water jar." The richness of the parables lies precisely in their volatility. They destabilize the single meanings and simple morals into which they have been imprisoned. They even challenge the simple slogans by which they have become known.

But the multiplicity of meaning contained in parables is further compounded by the situation of the listener. To understand—literally, "to stand under"—the weight of one of these stories, one has to know where one is standing in the first place. One of the most uncomfortable aspects of listening to parables is that they inevitably locate their listeners.

A friend working at a homeless shelter was leading a Bible study one night on the story of the healing of the leper from Matthew 8:1-4. She was retelling the parable and elaborating it for her audience. As she did, she became aware of an urgent energy in the room. When she came to the part of the story where Jesus touches the leper, touches the untouchable, the unclean one, and utters the words "Be clean!" the energy broke. It was as if Jesus, through the leper, had touched the homeless people in her congregation that night. How they longed for such contact!

She had led the same Bible study only a week before in her field work congregation to a more middle-class gathering. There the parable had made the people pensive, as they remembered the "untouchable" people in their own worlds, to whom they were being called to minister. Perhaps this group of listeners was even thinking about some of the homeless they had passed by in the streets that week, shedding not a glance. The people in the middle-class congregation had immediately identified with Jesus, the one who touched, and were thrown into thoughts of all those whom they had—or had not!—touched that week. The field work congregation had seen themselves immediately in Jesus, but the homeless people had seen themselves in the leper. How differently this healing story located the two audiences!

But the story also located its teller. My friend noticed the energy in the room, because she had not experienced it before. She had told and retold the story of healing to people like the ones in her field work congregation. These people identified with

Jesus, the healer, not with the lepers, the ones in need of healing. They considered themselves already healed. As my friend thought about this, she realized that she, as a pastor, identified herself with the healer. In the same instant, she also realized that her assumed identification with the healer in the story had closed down the possibility of any identification with those in need of healing and any acknowledgment of her own need for healing. In reading the story and constantly placing herself in the role of Jesus, she had consistently denied all those parts of her being in need of healing. She had consistently closed off all of the story's healing message for her. The story also located my friend.

The story—and the story of the story!—also locates me, in telling it, and the reader, in reading it. That I recount the story of the teacher and her two congregations, that I, like the biblical editors just alluded to, even give it that title or slogan, locates me as someone a little too comfortable with stationary meanings and single interpretations. I am willing to be surprised with alternative meanings, but—alas!—also quick to systematize even the surprises. How does the story locate you, dear reader?

Suddenly we are all onstage. Perhaps that is appropriate. Reading scripture is like watching a play that is produced as theater-in-the-round. An experienced cast plays to all points in the circle of spectators surrounding them. The spectator might wish to move around the theater along with the players, always positioning herself so as to catch the full force of the play. Failing that, she learns to watch the faces of others in the audience more strategically located, gleaning from their faces what they are better able to see. Gradually, she learns to register on her own face and in her own reactions the action on the stage, so that when the action onstage plays to her section of the theater, others may be able to see it on her face. Theater-in-the-round demands that the spectator participate with the players in this way. Theater-in-the-round demands that she watch, not only the stage, but the rest of the audience. Theater-in-the-round demands that she acknowledge vantage points other than her own, without relinquishing her own unique perspective, but knowing that it is not the only one. Theater-in-the-round demands that she move, if not in body, then certainly in imagination and attention.

Hearing scripture, listening to the parables, telling and

retelling them: These activities attend to a Word that is presented in the round. We sit inside a hermeneutical circle of performance, as attentive to the action that occurs onstage, as we are to the reactions of others in the audience. As we sit inside this parable of power by Robert Fulghum, we might ask the following questions: Who do I identify with in the parable of power? the one telling? the Mermaid? What about all the other "wired-up gradeschoolers"? the trusting parents? the trustworthy childcare provider? the other Mermaids who did not speak up? Would I have wanted to be a Giant, a Wizard, or a Dwarf? a Mermaid or a King? Would I have wanted to be a Sorceress? a Burro? The "right answers" to these questions inevitably escape us; the only truth is that parables inevitably locate both their tellers and their hearers. They read their readers. They tell us where we are—or aren't; they tell us who we are—or aren't. In this introductory chapter, I offer the story by Robert Fulghum as a parable, and I suggest that we walk around some of the various truths that the story might have for us and about us.

On Power

Further, I offer the story, not only as a parable, but as a parable about power. The question then becomes: What is power? A book could be written to address this question, and several already have.[3] Power has been variously interpreted as commodity, as capacity, and as relationship.

As commodity, power is external to the individual, a good that one accumulates, like land, money, knowledge, possessions, or people in one's debt. Because there are finite quantities of all of these commodities, power is seen to be a commodity that could be in potentially diminishing supply. Thus, in this interpretation, the more power one person possesses, the less there is available to others. The powerful have; the powerless have not. Power is played like a zero-sum game and regulated by the rules of the marketplace: competition, supply and demand, and whatever counts as "fair and equitable" exchange.

This kind of power operates not infrequently in meetings of churchfolk. Even among "priesthoods of all believers," some priests are more equal than others, and a superior power is measured in terms of ecclesiastical status (clergy, professional layperson, seminarian, educator, and so forth), education, profession, money, eloquence, or raw charisma. Meetings configure themselves around such figures, and people measure their own influence in terms of distance or proximity to these key figures. Rather than empower others, these figures often define a playing field, determine the game that will be played, and assign positions to the various players.

As capacity, power is seen to be an individual ability that can be used to dominate or to empower, to educate or to brainwash, to inspire or to control. Here power is defined as an ability to do or to create something. The justification for this understanding of "power" is buried in its etymological roots. "Power" is derived from the Latin verb *posse*, which means literally, "to be able to." In this interpretation, the powerful are those who are able to do something: the strong. The powerless are those who are unable to do something: the weak. Power is played like a barroom brawl or a schoolyard fight and regulated, at best, by conscience, at worst, by a conviction that "might makes right."

Nor is this understanding of power alien to churchly experience. It undergirds fundamental philosophies of leadership education in church and synagogue and among Protestant, Catholic, and Jew. Students for ministry are chosen on the basis of various capacities deemed appropriate to leadership: spiritual maturity, biblical literacy, confessional commitment, administrative ability, pastoral sensibilities, and so on. Seminary then hones, refines, and fine-tunes these capacities for positions of power within the church.

As relationship, power is seen broadly to describe kind and quality of interaction between people, animals, institutions, environments. This understanding of power acknowledges that power does not exist in a vacuum, without others with whom or over whom to exert itself. Attention then is given, not to what an individual has (power as commodity), nor to what the individual is (power as capacity), but to how the individual interacts with other persons or institutions and how power "circulates" among them. Michel Foucault elaborates:

> Power must be analysed as something which circulates, or rather as something which only functions in the form of a chain. It is never localised here or there, never in anybody's hands, never appropriated as a commodity or piece of wealth. Power is

employed and exercised through a net-like organisation. And not only do individuals circulate between its threads; they are always in the position of simultaneously undergoing and exercising this power. They are not only its inert or consenting target; they are always also the elements of its articulation. In other words, individuals are the vehicles of power, not its points of application.[4]

Understanding power as a "net-like organisation" demands a multifaceted interpretation of how various individuals and institutions figure into the complex web of relationships that constitute a life. In this interpretation, as Foucault hints, one simultaneously exercises power and undergoes its exercise. Because everyone is in a similar situation, the distinction between "powerful" and "powerless" becomes a situated distinction, which must be qualified by phrases like "in that moment," "in this situation," "in that exchange." Shifting moments, situations, and exchanges demand that one expect all analyses of power to be dynamic. Here power is regarded, not as capacity or possession of people or institutions, but as the subtle and ever-changing circumstances in which they interact as both objects and agents of its exercise.

This third definition of power is the one that resonates most clearly with people's experience of church life in particular and with our quotidian in general. People who possess large amounts of influence or wealth or status (power as commodity) are no less susceptible to being "used" or manipulated by the interests of others than are people who possess lesser amounts of influence or wealth or status. Power circulates; it does not gravitate either naturally or irresistibly toward those with cultural or ecclesial status. A brief look at the political history of the Vatican, Brazil, Czechoslovakia, local municipal politics, or denominational judicatories confirms that power circulates. Conversations with former students, now pastors, second this observation. Gifted with capacities they believed would make congregational leadership an easy burden, these new pastors now find themselves caught up in dynamics that completely baffle both their expectations and their education. They return to campus for continuing education asking where in the curriculum was the course "Congregational Dynamics"? Power circulates, and these new pastors have found that it has all too often circulated outside their expectations.

This book is for those former students who have so frequently returned with questions about power, authority, and how they might better exercise each. I confess a predisposition toward regarding power as a relationship, and the task of the book is to construct a series of relationships in which one might exercise power responsibly.

Playing the Parable of Power as Theater-in-the-Round

Having suggested what is intended by the words "parable" and "power," I now return to the parable of power with which I began this chapter. The story could have many names: "the parable of the Mermaid," "the parable of the Giants, Wizards, and Dwarfs," "the parable of the King of the Sea," "the parable of the King of Fools." Each name slants the story somewhat, binding us to one of its many meanings, blinding us to others. To catch more of the full force of the parable, I suggest we let it play theater-in-the-round and watch as its many meanings unfold.

The Powers of Leadership: Becoming an Agent

The character telling the story is not unlike a pastor or congregational leader, and as such, illustrates three critical aspects of all leadership in general, but of congregational leadership in particular:

1. the power to define a situation;
2. the power to name those involved in it;
3. the power to delineate space.

1) The Power of Defining

A leader possesses the power to define a situation; a leader can say what is going on. One of the expectations of a leader is that he will signal safety or danger for the community, that he will clarify or explain what may or may not be happening in the community.

A street person wandered into a small, urban congregation one Sunday during the sermon. Disheveled and disoriented, fidgeting and mumbling under his breath, he sat down in the last pew. Many of the parishioners turned their heads toward the commotion and shot various looks of disapproval back to the man, who, oblivious, continued fussing with his things. The parishioners turned back to the pastor, their anxious faces full of questions: Is this a "disturbance," a "disruption"? or should we consider this "normal"? What is going on? Their eyes sought silently some kind of definition of the situation.

The pastor kept on preaching as if nothing had happened. Gradually the congregation relaxed, and the mumbling and fidgeting of the visitor in the last pew relaxed into the rhythm of the sermon. By continuing her sermon undisturbed, by making the sermon large enough to embrace the commotion of this latecomer, the pastor indicated to the others that this was not a "disruption" or "disturbance." The pastor acted as if nothing were extraordinary. The church was "safe" for visitors, even noisy ones.

But the pastor's action also made it difficult for those in the congregation who *had* considered the presence of the street man an intrusion to approach her. She had defined the disruption as "normal." Anyone who challenged that definition would themselves be "abnormal." Her definition effectively closed down conversation with anyone in her congregation who might have wanted to question or to challenge her action.

Other actions were possible, each with its own effects. What would have happened if the pastor had motioned to an usher? What if she had broken away from her sermon, turning to address either the visitor or the congregation? What if she had become flustered in her delivery, lost in her sermon notes? The definitions given to the situation would have been quite different: Something here is amiss; something here is not normal; something here is inappropriate; something here is dangerous. The leader had the power to define the situation, to signal it as abnormal or to regard it as something entirely ordinary, even expected, in an urban congregation.

In Fulghum's story, the leader also possesses the power to define a situation, and this power of definition exists on various levels. The leader uses his power to create a game, "Giants, Wizards, and Dwarfs"; he explains to the children the purposes and ground rules of the game; he paces the game to hold their interest. When confronted with a creature quite insistent that she does not fit into the game as it is currently configured, he shifts his own position slightly and integrates her into the game quite easily.[5]

The power of definition is a power possessed by all leaders, whether they like it or not, whether they acknowledge it or not. In itself it is neither a positive nor a negative power. What, after all, would Fulghum have done with a roomful of eighty anxious and unhappy children, had he not created a kingdom and invited each of them to assume a fantastic identity? What image of the church would a congregation be left with, had a homeless man been bodily removed from the sanctuary during the pastor's sermon? What image was it left with, when the pastor continued her sermon as if nothing were extraordinary? This power of definition is one of the defining marks of leadership. Karen Lebacqz's remarks on the power of the professional can be extended to all leaders: "When we remember that professions deal with basic issues of human life such as relations to nature, others, and God, we begin to understand the tremendous power of definition possessed by the group that is given professional status."[6] The power of definition exists; it can be *used* positively or negatively.

A situation can be defined by either gesture or language. Gesture, or conscious body language, is more difficult to define, but one can be trained to notice it. In our culture, certain positions indicate openness: a relaxed body posture, arms apart, face intent. Other positions indicate defensiveness or defiance: a rigid stance, arms crossed, legs crossed, face frowning. The preacher's ability to continue her sermon nonplussed by the obvious interruptions of a homeless person in the midst of the congregation was a gesture of welcome to the man and a gesture of openness to her parishioners. Different gestures might have signaled denial or discomfort. What we cannot see in the Fulghum text is how he was standing, as he gave the orders to his troops: "You have to decide *now* which you are—a GIANT, a WIZARD, or a DWARF!" Those words could be accompanied by various and nefarious gestures, any one of which might invite disobedience, command immediate obedience, cause consternation, or evoke challenge. Apparently, Fulghum gave the command in such a way as to initiate "frenzied, whispered consultation" among the children, yet also invite at least one of them to challenge his categories. "Where do the Mermaids stand?"

Language also defines a situation. We see Fulghum creating a world in his naming. Through language he creates an imaginary, mythical landscape in which children are endowed with magical powers, the powers of giants, wizards, and dwarfs. The children did not have these powers before. In the naming, they are both endowed and experienced. But language also normalizes and limits. Fulghum's landscape was a terrestrial one, with no possibilities for aqueous worlds or sea creatures. The Mermaid's presence reminds him of these limitations, and Fulghum's immediate response is negation: "There are no such things as Mermaids." The creature of Mermaid does not fit the landscape he has created, and rather than change that landscape, his immediate reaction is to deny her existence. Language is a powerful shaper of reality, but the question then becomes: whose?

The power of a leader is not only to name, but also to ask precisely the question: whose? Who is doing the naming? A vivid example of this in ecclesial life today is churchly discussion of sexuality. Sexuality is defined as an "issue" by many of the larger Protestant denominations compelled to commission studies and issue papers on the subject.[7] The predominance of papers produced on this "issue" is staggering, and a leader must pause to ask, What does it mean to construe sexuality as an "issue," indeed, one of the biggest issues in American religious life?[8] French philosopher Michel Foucault noticed the current fascination with sexuality and asked:

> The central issue . . . is not to determine whether one says yes or no to sex, whether one formulates prohibitions or permissions, whether one asserts its importance or denies its effects, or whether one redefines the words one uses to designate it; but to account for the fact that it is spoken about, to discover who does the speaking, the positions and viewpoints from which they speak, the institutions which prompt people to speak about it and which store and distribute the things that are said.[9]

The power of definition in the church can be used to clarify and question, or to deny and delimit, but it always remains within the power of a leader to ask: How is the situation being defined? Who defined it? Whose story gets included? Whose story is problematized in this account?[10] Whose story gets left out of this account altogether?

2) The Power of Naming

In addition to the power of defining a situation, leaders possess a power to name those involved in it. The leaders can name themselves; they can name those around them. The whole process and product of naming shapes identity.

In this remembrance of the Quincentennial, we would do well to remember the power of naming. It can be an act of colonization, claiming, representing, and controlling an unknown landscape. In reading the journals of Christopher Columbus, one is struck with the power of naming.

[Sunday, October 28]. . . and the admiral understood that the ships of the Grand Khan come there, and that they are large; and that from there to the mainland it is ten days' journey. The admiral called that river and harbour *San Salvador.* [Monday, October 29] He weighed anchor from that harbour and navigated to the west in order, as he says, to go to the city where he thought that the Indians told him that the king resided. One point of the island ran out six leagues to the north-west; from there another point ran out to the east ten leagues. He went another league, and saw a river with a smaller mouth, to which he gave the name *Rio de la Luna.* He went on until the hour of vespers. He saw another river, much larger than the former, and so the Indians told him by signs, and near it he saw fair villages of houses. He called the river the *Rio de Mares.*[11]

The beautiful harbor, the river, and later the city are named in the language of the colonizer after a Christian saint. The naming bestows on the land a trinitarian blessing: It is baptized in the name of the explorer's God, in the name of his country, and in the name of his language. Indeed, the tone of the journal as a whole replicates, perhaps deliberately, the cadence of the creation narratives from Genesis—with the notable exception that Columbus did *not* observe the seventh day as a day of rest. But there is the same desire to bring order out of chaos, in this case a European order out of a perceived Indian chaos. Mary Louise Pratt comments, "Navigational mapping exerted the power of naming as well, of course. Indeed, it was in naming that the religious and geographical projects came together, as emissaries claimed the world by baptizing landmarks and geographical formations with Euro-Christian names."[12] It is not surprising that maps from these early centuries of exploration portrayed all manner of leviathans and sea monsters poking their ugly heads out of uncharted waters.

Resistance also is registered in a name. Rather than baptize the landscape with his own God, nation, and language, an early explorer of the Yucatan asked the indigenous peoples what they called their surroundings. They answered, "Yucatan," literally, "We don't know." The misunderstanding has been incorporated into five centuries of geographic maps of Central America.

The power in and of a name moved a congregation in the ethnically, racially, and religiously diverse city of San Francisco to change its name from "Christ Lutheran Church," a title quite common among churches in that denomination, to "Christ Church, Lutheran." In the transposition of adjectives the church intended to indicate an openness to all who considered themselves members of Christ's Church. Yet it signaled simultaneously that the confessional commitments and liturgical practice of that church were marked by that part of Christ's Church that called itself "Lutheran." Name configured a particular representation; a new name configured a new representation.

The power in and of a name prompted the question Jesus posed to his disciples: "Who do people say that I am?" After hearing the standard answers, he posed the question more directly: "And who do *you* say that I am?" Peter answered, with more wisdom than he knew, "You are the Christ, the Son of the living God."[13] That answer defined an identity, not only for the one named "the Christ," but decisively for the ones who followed the Christ and for the communities that recorded this saying. All three Synoptic Gospels—Matthew, Mark, and Luke—bestow upon Peter the confession of the Christ. In John's Gospel, the story does not appear. Rather, it is Mary Magdalene who is the first to confess the Christ. In John's Gospel, Peter's confession appears on her lips.

In the verses that follow Peter's confession in Matthew, Jesus' rejoinder to Simon Bar-Jona is to confer upon him a new name: Peter, or the rock. The naming is a new configuration of power, for the author of the Gospel has other words for Jesus to say: "You are Peter, and on this rock I will build my church, and the gates of Hades will not prevail against it. I will give you the keys of the kingdom of heaven, and whatever you bind on earth will be bound in heaven, and whatever you loose on earth will be loosed in heaven" (Matt. 16:18-19). The text gives Peter an authority apart from and over the other disciples. The text would ultimately be used to establish the supremacy of the community of worshipers that formed itself in Peter's name: the church at Rome.

Bishop of Rome, Callistus I (217–222 C.E.) was the first to invoke Petrine authority for his views in a controversy on penance. Later, Bishop Stephen I of Rome (254–257 C.E.) claimed that his succession from Peter established the "primacy" of Rome for all of Christendom. It was left to the Roman bishops Damasus (366–384 C.E.) and Leo I (440–461 C.E.) to provide more specific biblical and theological arguments for the primacy of their see.[14]

Throughout centuries of Judaism and Christianity, naming has had a unique power. As has been mentioned, the act of creation itself was an act of naming and distinction. "And God saw that the light was good; and God separated the light from the darkness. God called the light Day, and the darkness he called Night" (Gen. 1:4-5). The first human creature is given the task of naming the whole of creation. "So out of the ground the Lord God formed every animal of the field and every bird of the air, and brought them to the man to see what he would call them; and whatever the man called every living creature, that was its name. The man gave names to all cattle, and to the birds of the air, and to every animal of the field" (Gen. 2:19-20). It is a task and a text that have often been used to sanction domination of the whole of creation. Naming configures power. There is power in both the name and the one who bestows it.

It is in this biblical context of naming that the Christian rite of baptism is practiced. Ironically, the rite is popularly seen to confer upon a child the family name. Theologically, however, the practice means something almost the opposite. Baptism bestows upon the child, not some euphonious or strategic combination of first, middle, and family appellations, but the far more radical title "child of God." Far from the christening for which it is often mistaken, baptism gives an infant or adult a new name, "child of God," and integrates the infant or adult into a new family, the family of the children of God. For an early Christian martyr, the noblewoman Perpetua, the name of Christian defined a family quite different from her kinship families. In prison, awaiting the arena, she is depicted as severing connections with both her aristocratic father and her infant son, a representation of a new "family" and a new identity for those who bore the name "Christian."[15]

Naming plays an important role in the tiny parable of power by Fulghum. He names three groups of mythical creatures—Giants, Wizards, and Dwarfs—and allows the children the choice of belonging to one of them. He is clear about the purpose of the game: "achieving consensus on group identity," which is truly "no mean accomplishment." He is troubled at first by the presence of a Mermaid, one who did not fit into the paradigm he had configured, and his immediate response is that there are no Mermaids. Impressed with her persistence, however, he finally admits her into the kingdom. Yet, even and especially in this gesture of welcome, he retains sovereignty. He names himself King of the Sea, a title that simultaneously colonizes and masters her home.

The turn is both lovely and terrifying. The leader does not press her to choose among the three options he had offered—Giants, Wizards, and Dwarfs. He allows her to remain a Mermaid, one who does not "fit into the scheme of things"—at least not into *his* scheme of things. He permits her to retain her identity. At the same time—and this is quite terrifying!—he does not acknowledge that he is the one who created the "scheme of things," the distinction between "similarity" and "difference," that he created the "norm" and all that qualifies as "normal," and that he himself constructed all the categories, except the one which he initially refuses to recognize. The leader is not really cognizant of the range of his powers. Nor has he asked whether it is really consonant with the identity of a Mermaid to *stand*. She might well have preferred swimming!

How has the power of naming been used in this situation? Obviously, Fulghum thinks he has done "the right thing": acknowledging the uniqueness of this aqueous creature, yet retaining his control over the situation. That is his task. She has, after all, along with seventy-nine other children, been entrusted to his care. He has derived an ingenious manner of holding eighty children loosely but firmly in his grasp—no mean feat! From his perspective and probably the parents' as well, he has indeed done "the right thing." But to regard the story as parable is to admit many different perspectives into the mix: the perspective of the Mermaid, the perspective of the shy Griffin who did not ask for definition from the King of the Sea but quietly decided to masquerade for the afternoon in Dwarf's clothing, the perspective of a Burro who was stunned entirely by the finery of such mythical masks and escaped into the game unnoticed, the perspective of the absent parents, the perspective of the King who felt like a Fool, the perspectives of others whom I invite you to name and to invent.

Naming may be variously used to constitute new systems of power or reinforce old ones, to construct or deconstruct identities, but it always remains the responsibility of a leader to ask, What names are being used here, for me and for others? Who has given the names? Is every name one that the person so designated would freely choose? Is there in fact the freedom to choose the name each one would so wish?

3) The Power of Delineating Space

Space is a critical vehicle for power, as any who have tried to reconfigure worship space have discovered! Many altars are on raised platforms and up against the wall, a powerful statement of the presence and power of God. God is somehow above, apart from, and other. Parishioners watch the backs of their pastors, immobile under layers of liturgical vestments, as the elements are consecrated and prayers offered. A free-standing altar makes a different statement about the presence and power of God: God is in our midst. Surrounding a free-standing altar, parishioners watch one another as the elements are consecrated and prayers offered. The way worship space is arranged configures power.

Space configures power in other ways, for space is fluid. A pastor related the experience of delivering a sermon away from a pulpit, into which he had to climb and which was already situated in a chancel raised several steps above the floor of the nave.

> When I didn't ascend into the pulpit, as I had every Sunday for the past four years, I could sense the excitement. People were all eyes and all ears, as I stood in the middle of the chancel and began the sermon. But when I began moving slowly down the steps into the nave and walking down the aisle, talking all the time, things really broke loose. I could feel people physically moving in the seats away from the aisle!

The dramatic impact of innovation is always palpable—and not entirely welcome. At coffee hour afterward, the pastor noted that comments were mixed. Some parishioners made strong suggestions that he return to his sermonic perch in subsequent Sundays. They had fixed in their minds where the "holy" was located in the sanctuary, and they did not want that place to be changed. For them the pastor's movements constituted a violation of that holy space, and they were not eager to choose between reconfiguring their understanding of the "holy" and watching as the "holy" was violated. For others, however, the pastor's movements were inviting, reminding them that the Word of God was for their ears, representing the presence of that Word in their midst. They welcomed a shift in worship space and a dynamic interpretation of the "holy."

We have difficulty expressing our relationship to something so subtle and pervasive as space. On one hand, people tend to take space for granted—unless it is taken away. Yet, for those who have no space, who have no place of their own, space—or the lack thereof—is crucial. Brazilian peasants rendered homeless by the influx of multinational corporations experience the displacement of having their land taken away from them.[16] Exodus and the promised land are prominent themes in Latin American liberation theologies. Similarly, African people brought to North America as slaves were wrenched from their homelands, their cultures, their religions, and transported into a country in which they were literally "nobodies" with "no place." Gradually, as the memory of Africa faded, the feeling of "displacement" became constitutive of African American identity. Their resistance remains in their songs, where they created space for themselves and their God.

> My God is a rock in a weary land
> My God is a rock in a weary land
> My God is a rock in a weary land
> Shelter in time of storm.[17]

Writer Yi-Fu Tuan observes that space is usually taken for granted. It is difficult to talk about:

People tend to suppress that which they cannot express. If an experience resists ready communication, a common response among activists ("doers") is to deem it private—even idiosyncratic—and hence unimportant. In the large literature on environmental quality, relatively few works attempt to understand how people feel about space and place, to take into account the different modes of experience (sensorimotor, tactile, visual, conceptual), and to interpret space and place as images of complex—often ambivalent—feelings.[18]

Yet Tuan's point—and indeed his life's work—was to put into words and under analysis how space affects people's lives and the way in which they experience things. Michel Foucault has carried this attention to space one step farther by analyzing the relationship between space and power. Foucault notes the privileged status given to time and history in the nineteenth and twentieth centuries: "Space was treated as the dead, the fixed, the undialectical, the immobile. Time, on the contrary, was richness, fecundity, life, dialectic."[19] Trying in his work to redress this imbalance, Foucault argues that space configures power and is fundamental to any exercise of power.[20] As a striking example of the way in which space configures power, Foucault turns, in *Discipline and Punish*, to the design of Jeremy Bentham's model prison, the Panopticon. The prison is constructed in a circle with all cells looking out onto a guard tower at the center of the circle. The only windows in the cell are the windows facing the guard tower, and the guard tower has windows all around it. The prisoner never knows precisely whether or not the guard is looking at him, but he has the impression that he is under constant surveillance.[21]

Space configures power in the Fulghum story in quite interesting ways. The leader creates order out of chaos much in the way that the author of Genesis records order emerging from chaos: by distinguishing and separating different elements, one from another. The acts of distinction and separation are spatially configured: the leader assigns space to the Giants, the Wizards, and the Dwarfs. He creates a terrestrial universe full of magical powers and mythical beings. The Mermaid accosts him, because there is no place left for her. "Where do the Mermaids stand?"

It is a surprising question posed to a King who had until that point considered his kingdom to be entirely terrestrial. Suddenly he is discovered by an entirely other and aqueous kingdom, of which he had not known. Suddenly he is discovered by an entirely new kind of creature, of whom he had not known. The King's first reaction is denial: "There are no Mermaids." But then, recovering quickly, he colonizes. He usurps the new territory and appoints himself King of the Sea as well and ruler of all creatures therein, as he had been King of the Land and ruler of all Giants, Wizards, and Dwarfs. He grants the Mermaid a "place" to stand beside him.

Telling the story as he does, Fulghum only reinforces his power to delineate space. While she does not accept his categories of being, the Mermaid does accept his power of delineating space. She asks him to recognize her as she is; she also asks him for a place to "stand." In so doing, she literally "understands" him and his power in the sense of "standing under" him. Becoming a subject to him, that is, a Mermaid and not a Dwarf or a Wizard, is also becoming subject to him. She wants him to find her a place. In telling the story, Fulghum consolidates that power. But think of the stories he cannot tell: the story of the shy Griffin who did not need an adult either to recognize him or to assign him a place, but was content to masquerade as a Dwarf for the afternoon, the story of the Burro who found his adult caretaker to be entirely irrelevant and escaped into the game unnoticed.

Space is a vector of power ever present in any given situation. It remains the responsibility of the leader to ask, Who has arranged the space? Who are the kings of sea and land? Who has appointed them? Who delineated the boundaries? Are they flexible or inflexible? Who defends the boundaries and how? Does everyone have a place to stand? Does anyone need a place to swim? What are we doing *here?*

Reflection Questions:

Defining, naming, and delineating space: These all fall within the power of a leader. The leader should at all times and in all places be aware of her ability to define, name, and delineate space. But even in those times and those places where she has not initiated the definitions, the names, and the configurations of spaces, it is always her responsibility to ask the questions these capacities raise:

1. How is the situation defined? Who defined it? Does this definition allow for greatest ambiguity and flexibility?
2. What names have been given? *to* whom? *by* whom? Would these be names the individuals so named would themselves have chosen?
3. Who has arranged the space? Does everyone have a place to stand, to swim, to sit within it?
4. What is the community's self-understanding, implicit or explicit? Is everyone here?

In short, every leader must be prepared and be on the lookout for Mermaids. More important, every leader must be prepared to find a place for the Mermaids to stand. But most important of all, every leader must be prepared to learn to swim.

The Powers Acting on a Leader

Our first consideration illustrated three aspects of the power of leadership: the power to define a situation, the power to name, and the power to delineate space. The illustrations and anecdotes argue experientially the truth of these powers.

Yet, there is another truth as well. If people are simultaneously exercising and undergoing the exercise of power, then we must consider not only the powers that a leader has, but the powers that a leader undergoes. Put differently, while all leaders possess power, all leaders are also possessed by power. They operate in structures and networks of power to which they are themselves subject. All leaders have the capacity to create structures of power, but they are simultaneously caught up in structures of power, which exercise power on them.[22] In the first consideration, we looked at how leaders exercise power. Now, we turn to the ways in which even and especially leaders "undergo" power. Two aspects of the power that exercises itself upon leaders are critical:

1. Authority: the power of legitimation and legitimating institutions

2. Community: the power of those who are being led

Authority

Those readers who remember the 1960s, remember a popular slogan from that decade: "Question authority!" That slogan fueled another: "Don't trust anyone over thirty!" Those around in the sixties remember the passion with which each of these imperatives was uttered. The negative energy buttresses Richard Sennett's claim that authority is one of the emotional bonds of society.[23] We could no more imagine a society without it than we could think of living without air. Authority is "the emotional expression of power."[24] Like power, it is in itself neither good nor bad; the question is to its use and its duration.

Authority is often defined as "legitimate" power. It is power that is externally recognized, publicly validated, and often institutionally conferred. These three adjectives—external, public, institutional—define the power that also circulates as authority.

First, authority is always external to the one possessing it. It comes from outside the individual, though it may resonate with interior gifts. Jesus was "one who spoke with authority," and everyone noticed it. But then the question became: But by what authority does he speak? by whose authority does he work miracles? Authority that emanates completely from within the one who speaks and works miracles is usually referred to as "personal authority" or charisma, and charismatic figures run the gamut from saintliness to demagoguery, from Mother Teresa to Adolf Hitler. In this book, we shall refer to "personal authority" as charisma, reserving "authority" to refer to externally legitimated power.

Many seminarians feel an interior "call" to engage in ordained ministry, but this alone is not enough to be ordained. The "call" to ordained ministry must also come from outside the seminarian, confirming her own internal authority. This confirmation takes place over time, through prayer and discernment, interview and examination, testing and questioning. The denomination takes a vigorous role in this whole confirmation process, placing a seminarian "in care" of a candidacy or fellowship committee and often requiring written and oral examinations, in addition to psychological testing. In established denominations, the process is long and involved, but it attests to the external character of power that a leader wields.

Even within a congregation, there is external validation of lay leadership. Often a nominating committee will choose persons who it feels could do a good job in a particular service within the church. Their potential is externally recognized and called into action. This is even true of the leader in our Fulghum story. He was, as he himself notes, "left in charge" of a large number of children. He did not advertise himself and his abilities; he was deemed by the absent parents to be an adequate childcare provider. His abilities were externally validated. The parents voluntarily and trustingly left their children with him.

Second, authority is always publicly recognized, whether formally or informally. Formal public recognition of authority usually takes the form of a rite or ritual. The inauguration of the President of the United States involves a public recognition of his power, both on the part of the citizenry and on the part of global powers and principalities. The ordination of a minister or deacon or the installation of a church council member or elder is a public recognition of the initiate's power.

An essential part of each of these rites is the making of promises, and those promises form networks of accountability. In each of these ceremonies, promises are made between the person and the office to which that person has been called, between the person and the community, and finally between the person and God. In some instances, these promises are reflexive. For example, while the ordinand or deacon pledges fidelity to the congregation, the congregation simultaneously affirms its fidelity in return. The fact that each of these ceremonies happens in the presence of God—even the President of the United States rests his hand on a Bible as he is sworn in—acknowledges a divine presence and an awareness of the fidelity God extends to both person and office. Promise making creates the fragile tendrils of connection that hold communities together—often in spite of themselves. Hannah Arendt reminds us that promise making always stands firmly against a human tendency toward unpredictability: "The basic unreliability of men who can never guarantee today who they will be tomorrow, and . . . the impossibility of foretelling the consequences of an act within a community of equals where everybody has the same capacity to act."[25] It is hoped we become the people we have promised to be, with the help of God and the community of people who have pledged to support us.

Informal public recognition of authority often does not get ritual attention. One who "speaks with authority" is usually recognized informally by the size of the crowd one can draw. In a German university, that informal recognition is usually publicly stated in the size of the lecture hall a professor may be expected to fill. Formal public recognition has already been given in rituals of inaugural lectures and formal instatement into the faculty. In a congregation, informal recognition is given in the number of pews filled on any given Sunday or the spaces vacant in a Tuesday morning Bible study class. Formal public recognition has already been given in rituals of ordination and installation.

Fulghum probably had a kind of informal authority: being "left in charge" of eighty children of grade-school age attests either to his skill as a childcare provider or to a generic desperation on the part of the parents. Whichever, he is informally acknowledged to be someone worthy of being left in charge of young children.

Finally, authority is often institutionally conferred. Rituals are often, but not always, the institution's way of inducting someone into its structures and articulating the mutual accountability that holds all parties in place. The licensing of counselors, psychiatrists, or psychotherapists is another way of conferring institutional authority upon someone. The rostering of clergy, the commissioning of lay professionals, the installation of church council, vestry, or cabinet are its ecclesiastical counterparts. Often, licensing or rostering makes explicit a professional's rights and obligations to the conferring institution.

Often an ordained minister is held institutionally accountable by vows sworn at her ordination, but also by various juridical documents outlining conduct becoming the office of the ordained minister. These documents outline what constitutes conduct not deemed fitting for the clergy, expectations for financial accountability, and confessional integrity. The documents remind leaders that they are a larger system of power and that, even as they faithfully exercise their power in leadership, they undergo the faithful exercise of power that an institution wields on behalf of the mission of the church in the world.

Authority, or legitimate power, is surely one of the most important "emotional bonds" of today's society. As such, it is both necessary and ambivalent, from both an institutional and a personal point of view.

From an institutional point of view, the exercise of authority is ambivalent. On one hand, the institution has a responsibility to itself and those whom it serves to monitor the quality and practices of its leaders. There is evidence of flagrant institutional abuse in the increasing evidence of clergy sexual abuse. Here, leaders were using their institutional authority to do great damage. The institution must exercise its authority to protect people from excesses of its leaders. Standards of conduct and practice are crucial. On the other hand, institutions are often frightened by what is destabilizing and off center. Standards engender conformity and erase voices of critique or dissent.

In defiance of the church's stated policy prohibiting the ordination of openly gay and lesbian persons, two San Francisco Lutheran churches called a lesbian couple and a gay male. Faced with a similar official position in the Presbyterian church, a congregation in metropolitan New York called an openly lesbian woman as pastor.[26] Located on opposite sides of the country, these congregations share in a spirit of "ecclesiastical disobedience" in challenging the authority of their institutions. All three congregations would probably agree that an institution has both the right and the responsibility to set standards for its leadership. This aspect they are not challenging. Rather, they challenge the kinds of standards set by their respective institutions and the way in which these standards are used, which to their minds violate justice and deprive the churches of much-needed leadership.

From the personal point of view of the leader, the exercise of authority is ambivalent. On one hand, institutional authority, provided it is exercised justly, is the backing for difficult decisions and tough situations. In addition, it is an ever-present reminder that the leader is not operating in a vacuum. She is part of a larger whole and fits into the integrity of a larger whole. On the other hand, institutional authority can put constraints on a leader's ability actually to accomplish anything. More seriously, institutional authority can often force a leader or a congregation to take a stand on conscience in opposition to procedures and policies it believes to be unjust and against the larger mandates of the gospel, as did the aforementioned three congregations who called openly gay and lesbian pastors, despite institutional censure. Karen Lebacqz calls this tension between the need for institutional backing and the constraints it places on one's leadership a "paradox of power": "As a professional, the minister is still powerful and is expected to exercise authority. . . . Yet at the same time, their power is undercut by the structures in which they work. They are both powerful and not powerful."[27] The "paradox of power" reminds the leader that her leadership is always part of a larger network of power and a larger structure of authority within which she operates and which operates on her. This larger structure of authority is the necessary reminder of a greater accountability; it can also simultaneously act as an invitation to conformity.

Community

The community figures significantly in the network of power within which one exercises leadership. Community can serve either to enhance or to destroy the capabilities of its leaders. Philosopher Hannah Arendt goes so far as to say that there is no real power outside a community; there is only tyranny. Power is not an individual possession, but a group phenomenon.

> [Power] belongs to a group and remains in existence only so long as the group keeps together. When we say of somebody that he is "in

power" we actually refer to his being empowered by a certain number of people to act in their name. The moment the group, from which the power originated to begin with (*potestas in populo*, without a people or group there is no power), disappears, "his power" also vanishes.[28]

Simply put, Arendt emphasizes that there are no leaders without community; only with the acknowledgment of a community can anyone lead in the first place. Consonant with her understanding of "power" as a corporate phenomenon, she juxtaposes "power" with tyranny, which depends on the ability of the tyrant to isolate people one from another through the social mechanisms of fear, suspicion, and surveillance. Despite the fact that they do not trust the tyrant, such subjects will never trust *one another* enough to discover, engage, and exercise their corporate "power," and they will be forever governed by force, violence, and coercion.[29] Thus, it is not the "power" of the unjust tyrant which is at issue in situations of oppression. As far as Arendt is concerned, the tyrant has no power; the tyrant has only the instruments of death, and these are never powerful enough to subdue the "power" of people acting in concert. What is at issue for Arendt in a situation of oppression is the corporate character of power. When the subjects begin to trust one another and act in concert, they will *create* the power necessary to overthrow force, violence, coercion, and the most sinister of tyrants.

Such a concerted exercise might even create the power necessary to disfranchise a day-care leader. Suppose in response to Fulghum's declaration of the game, his troops had "huddled in frenzied, whispered consultation," but then emerged to make a calm counterproposal: "Sorry, your Highness. But the game *we* want to play is Griffins, Unicorns, and Dragons." The power of the leader would have been utterly defused, and he would have to exert his will by force, threat, or coercion: "Quite the contrary. The game we are *going* to play is Giants, Wizards, and Dwarfs, and anyone who doesn't want to play will be sent outside in the rain to pick up trash around the property." Suppose in response to Fulghum's welcoming, but perhaps patronizing remark to the Mermaid—"The Mermaid stands right here by the King of the Sea"—the Mermaid had replied, "You don't understand, sir. There are no Kings in the Sea; there are only Mermaids. And if you wish to relate to us, you must first learn to swim."

37

The statement would have confronted and challenged his power. We can see why the King would wish to give the Mermaid a place to stand close beside him, lest any of the other Giants, Wizards, and Dwarfs get wind of her subversion and attempt more creative identities for themselves. We can see the risk Fulghum took in acknowledging the Mermaid in the first place. It would have been far easier to say: "Look, I don't care *who* you really are. For the next two hours you're going to be either a Giant or a Wizard or a Dwarf. And that's final."

Arendt's discussion of a power that flows from the community to the leader emphasizes the importance of the network of power which encompasses both leader and community. For the leader, this can be a mixed blessing. On one hand, she might be pushed to grow into the needs and missions of the community. Time and again, I have heard pastors say of a congregation, "I learned so much there . . ." or "That's where I really learned what stewardship/Christian caring/discipleship was all about." These people have felt challenged and stretched by their congregations; they know whence their "power" came.

Fulghum also acknowledges the challenge presented to him by the Mermaid. She expanded his world, and his recognition of that is the beauty of the story. "It is not true, by the way, that mermaids do not exist. I know at least one personally. I have held her hand." His ability to see her world illumined his own and afforded him a glimpse of the world of all those who do not fit; as he puts it, "all those who are different, who do not fit the norm and who do not accept the available boxes and pigeonholes." The illumination may seem faint to those who dwell in an entirely aqueous realm and chafe at being expected to stand, when they'd much rather be swimming. But to those who inhabit the land, any acknowledgment of a world beyond the expanse of their known kingdoms could be enormously threatening.

On the other hand, there is the possibility of a phenomenon which Arendt does not acknowledge. Often a leader can be held captive to the desires and wishes of a community. The community can "empower" or "disempower" as it is pleased or displeased with the leader's performance. Again, this can be a "paradox of power" in which the designated leader is really powerless, enslaved to the will of the people she leads.

Perhaps it was the acuity of a leader who knew whence his

power came that made Pontius Pilate turn the decision of whom to crucify entirely over to the angry crowd that had gathered in front of him. The gospel of Matthew, the only Gospel to use the word "church" *(ekklesia)*, graphically and quite negatively represents the power of the crowd:

> The governor again said to them, "Which of the two do you want me to release for you?" And they said, "Barabbas." Pilate said to them, "Then what should I do with Jesus who is called the Messiah?" All of them said, "Let him be crucified!" Then he asked, "Why, what evil has he done?" But they shouted all the more, "Let him be crucified."
>
> So when Pilate saw that he could do nothing, but rather that a riot was beginning, he took some water and washed his hands before the crowd, saying, "I am innocent of this man's blood; see to it yourselves." Then the people as a whole answered, "His blood be on us and on our children!" (Matt. 27:21-25)[30]

Writing on the relationship between crowds and power, Elias Canetti comments on the speed, elation, and conviction of a baiting crowd. "It is the excitement of blind men who are blindest when they suddenly think they can see."[31]

We can only imagine the blindness of a room full of Giants, Wizards, and Dwarfs, had the groups decided to exercise more diabolical powers. Suppose in response to Fulghum's suggested game, the crowd had said: "Oh, but sir, the game we want to play is Burn-Down-the-Church," or "Terrorize-All-the-Youngest-Children," or "Overthrow-the-King-of-the-Sea!" There would be potentially dangerous issue in any one of these imaginary scenarios. But these various scenarios, real, imaginary, and biblical, confirm the considerable and ambivalent power of a community.

Authority and community: These are part of the network of power relations in which leaders are caught up. They exercise power on the leader. Along with the powers of leadership, they are part of the complex network of power in which leaders and communities find themselves.

The Exercise of "Power from on High"

Even if we know *what* powers emerge in leadership, both the powers that a leader exercises and the powers that operate upon a leader, we are often perplexed by the exercise of these powers.

Given the reality of this complex network of power, how might power be exercised? The question becomes even more nuanced, when we think of power in Christian contexts and Christian communities. How might Christian leaders exercise power? We worship the one whose strength was made perfect in weakness, the one whose power was revealed in powerlessness. How are *we* to exercise power? Perhaps we get some insight into an answer from various ways in which God exercises power.

> Thus it is written, that the Messiah is to suffer and to rise from the dead on the third day, and that repentance and forgiveness of sins is to be proclaimed in his name to all nations, beginning from Jerusalem. You are witnesses of these things. And see, I am sending upon you what my Father promised; so stay here in the city until you have been clothed with power from on high. (Luke 24:46b-49)

". . . until you have been clothed with power from on high." This is a text often read at ordination and commissioning services; it's a text that stirs hearts, engenders purpose, and serves as both inspiration and challenge for the future. But how will this power be translated into actual leadership in ministry?

". . . until you have been clothed with power from on high." I preached on this text at a seminary baccalaureate service not long ago, and I could feel the Spirit's presence in the chapel, because of and in spite of my own words of interpretation. I saw on the faces of the students a look of rapt appropriation: they were themselves being emboldened to take up this "power from on high." Some would be ordained; some would not. Whether churchworkers or ordained ministers in daily life, all would be serving in some leadership capacity in the church. What would their various ministries look like?

". . . until you have been clothed with power from on high." As inspiring as it is to think about being "clothed with power from on high," it is a good deal more difficult to exercise that power within a living, breathing, struggling congregation. The translation of a "power from on high" into "power within the office" is rugged indeed. And there are several reasons for the difficulty in translation.

First, with the conferral of this "power from on high" comes the distinct commission to be "servant to all." How do servanthood and power mix? Second, it is politics and not ecclesiology that is regarded as the "science of power." Insofar as church and state are, at least in the North American political and ecclesial traditions, separate, shouldn't the church leave power to the politicians and devote itself to service, or *diakonia*, instead? Third, power is a new experience, particularly for those who have traditionally considered themselves powerless: women and minority people in leadership roles. They both desire and are suspicious of an office and an authority that confers on them a power that has oppressed them and people like them. How do power and powerlessness mix? Finally, the gospel of Luke is talking about a kind of spiritual power descending on the disciples. Our immediate referents for talking about power are various secular definitions, definitions that largely define power as "power over" someone or something else, power as control, domination, and oppression. How do secular and theological definitions of power intersect?

Secular Understandings of Power

Power is a consistent topic of conversation in circles both sacred and secular and among groups that fall into categories of both "the powerful" and "the powerless." The "powerful" write about power, seeking to understand and to justify the power they hold. The "powerless" write about the subject, seeking to name the power of oppressed peoples. Most of these discussions hold one thing in common. They highlight a prominent definition of power as "power over" someone or something else. But is this dominant definition the only one?

Other approaches to power are beginning to surface. Post-Machiavellian administrators are rethinking their traditional "power over" strategies and tactics and looking at other options. A British theorist of the 1930s, Mary Parker Follett, distinguishes between "power over" and "power with" or coercive power and coactive power.[32] Seeking to understand the mysterious and irrational power that emanates from some religious leaders, sociologist Max Weber talks about charismatic power or "power within."[33] Feminists from a variety of disciplines have rejected "power over" as patriarchal; they have chosen instead the power of friendship, or "power with," as a form of liberating power.[34]

The cumulative work of these political philosophers, business administrators, sociologists, anthropologists, and feminists suggests three balanced ways of thinking about power: "power over," "power within" or charismatic power, and "power with," friendship or coactive power.

Theological Understandings of Power

Given this emerging trinity of secular understandings—"power over" or dominative power, "power within" or charismatic power, and "power with" or friendship, what are theological understandings of power which might form, inform, and transform each of these secular understandings of power? Perhaps the most important referent is the Trinity itself. It is within the Trinity that we understand the divine and dynamic equilibrium embedded in deity. A God who creates, judges, and preserves is also a God who is with us in the incarnation. This person of God informs how one exercises "power over." A God who sustains, surprises, reveals is also a God who enables and requires the kind of discernment necessary to distinguishing between God's Spirit and our own. This person of God informs how one exercises "power within." A God with us, "emmanuel," who befriends, comforts, and challenges, is also a God who shows us how to befriend one another. This person of God informs how one exercises "power with."

Reflection Questions

The strategy of this book, then, is bifocal and transformative. I propose to read secular theories of power in view of the Trinity to understand how power might be used faithfully and appropriately for leadership in ministry. I propose to examine each of these three forms of power and see how each might form, inform, and possibly even transform our own leadership in the churches.

1. What is each form of power and what are its salient characteristics, assets, and liabilities?
2. What does leadership in this mode look like?
3. What images of God could be used to justify and to challenge this form of power?
4. Finally, how might a theological understanding of power be used to transform this kind of power?

Power I

Power Over
Sovereignty, Parenthood,
or Bureaucracy

The Music Minister and the Preacher

"I grew up in a rural town in the East and still consider it home. I worked there, went to school there, and enjoyed the large circle of friends and family that I'd accumulated there. At 18 I entered the music program at one of the second largest church colleges in my denomination. At 21 I was licensed as a minister of music in that denomination. This gave me the authority to preach and to perform marriages.

"While checking the job listings one afternoon in the music department, I noticed a vacancy for a minister of music at a church about 45 miles away from my college in a little mining town called Connor's Corner. I actually had been to the town before. It was a small town, with a population of middle-/upper-middle class people who'd been miners, managers, and executives in the mine. I called the number listed and found myself talking to the preacher of Connor's Corner Community Church, Robert. We arranged to meet and discuss the position.

"Robert was about 40 years old, married with two children. He needed someone to direct the adult, youth, and children's choirs. The adult choir sang every Sunday; the youth choir, every three months; the children's choir, only on special occasions. Each choir met once a week: the adult choir on Wednesday nights, and the youth and children's choirs on Sunday evenings. Robert told me that 'in matters of worship, my word is final.' At the time, I remember thinking that that seemed appropriate. What interested me more was his sense that 'something needed to happen' with the youth and children's choirs.

"I suggested that we meet once a week to discuss any worship matters or pastoral problems either of us was aware of that might impinge on the ministry of the other. Robert agreed. I don't think that either of us anticipated any problems. Robert said he would convey the information to the deacons, who were meeting that week, and that he would recommend my appointment. He didn't foresee any difficulties with the appointment and assured me that there would be no problems with the hiring. As far as he was concerned, I could start work immediately.

"I remember wondering what an interview with the deacons might be like. But Robert seemed confident, and I found that reassuring. No written contract was forthcoming, nor would one have been customary for either the position or the denomination. Had I asked for one, I probably would not have gotten the job. Had I been offered one, I probably would not have taken the job. It would have made me suspicious of a church that worked so legalistically. I liked the idea of trusting the word of this older man. As Robert said, the deacons approved his choice. I started work immediately. On my first Sunday I sang a solo, and Robert introduced me to the congregation as 'Brother Kevin, our new minister of music.' I began rehearsing with the choirs that same week.

"I quickly got caught up in the life of the congregation. I did indeed have free rein over everything that had to do with music in the congregation, and that gave me a lot of energy and enthusiasm. I felt like I was well-received by members of the congregation of all ages, but particularly those who had younger children. I almost always had an invitation to Sunday dinner after the worship services and before the Sunday evening choir rehearsals. Robert and his wife, Lydia, who was a member of the adult choir, even invited me to dinner a few times. She was very sweet, and he was always cordial, if somewhat aloof. He didn't seem to get along well with children—even his own children! I wasn't sure whether he thought I fit into the category of 'child' or 'adult.' In some ways, he was remarkably like my father. I assumed that anything short of direct conflict constituted a good working relationship.

"I took my role as 'minister' of music quite seriously. I worked hard with all the choirs, typically beginning each rehearsal with a prayer and meditation that focused on the lyrics of the music we'd be practicing. Then we'd rehearse the music for the upcoming Sunday, work on some new music, and conclude by going over the music for the next Sunday.

"As minister of music, too, I had a prominent place in the

worship space of the congregation. On Sundays Robert would be on the right side of the chancel area, and I took my place on the left. Behind both of us was the choir. In front of and between us was the pulpit. The altar was down several steps in front of the pulpit in the nave.

"After about a month at Connor's Corner, Robert asked me to take on responsibility for the entire youth program. Since I'd been at the church, attendance in the youth choir had grown from three to about eight or twelve on any given Sunday. Already, I'd received a lot of encouragement from parents: 'We're so glad you're getting our kids involved in church again.' 'They're suddenly enjoying singing!' It seemed entirely appropriate that Robert would ask if I'd be in charge of the youth. At the time, he said quite plainly that he did not enjoy working with kids. Aside from this request, our weekly meetings were brief and business-like. Gradually, they dwindled to monthly meetings. This did not particularly alarm me. As I said, I assumed that anything short of direct conflict was OK. I guess I just sort of trusted that if Robert heard anything negative, he'd pass it on to me. No news was good news, and I was having a good time.

"In retrospect, I see that this increasing distance between us constituted a gradual breakdown in communication. But at the time, it did not disturb me. Robert and I had, after all, very different compasses for our ministries. Robert worked more with the deacons and the elderly, more established members of the congregation. I worked with the children, the youth, and those people directly involved in their care: their mothers. I assumed that Robert had a more laissez-faire style of management. I remember wanting a little more support from him. I wanted him to be as excited about my ministry as I was. But that just didn't seem to be his way.

"Things were going smoothly in the church as Christmas approached. All of the choirs were preparing special music for the holiday. I would leave shortly before the holiday to spend Christmas with my family in another part of the state, and the deacons had chosen the third Sunday in Advent as a time for special music. For me, it was a busy time, with end-of-semester pressures at college and extra rehearsals at church for all three choirs.

Baptistery

Choir (banked risers)

Rails

Preacher

Pulpit

Choir Director

Steps

Altar

"In the Wednesday night adult choir I had been working for the past three months on a very difficult piece of music: Dave Brubeck's 'La Fiesta de la Posada.' Brubeck, a well-known jazz musician, had recently become a Christian and begun writing sacred music. The piece had been performed at my college for its centennial celebration, and all denominational judicatories had been there. Given the strength and range of the adult choir, I thought it would be fun to try the piece out at Connor's Corner. I borrowed scores of the music from the college. I knew the piece would be challenging, but I thought we could do it. We began to rehearse early in the fall.

"I'd begun rehearsals for the Brubeck piece the same way I began to rehearse any new piece of music: with prayer and meditation on the lyrics. I focused on a different verse each week and spoke about how the text tied both sacred and secular meanings of Christmas together in a song of thanksgiving.

I remember that several choir members commented on the lyrics and thanked me for emphasizing that the celebration of Christ's birth did not have to exclude secular expressions of the holiday.

"The choir struggled more with Brubeck's syncopation and harmony, than with the lyrics. But we mastered the piece quickly and were having a lot of fun singing it. Robert's wife, Lydia, who sang in the adult choir, shared the enthusiasm of the group, and I left my last rehearsal before the third Sunday in Advent excited.

"On the Sunday of the performance, I arrived at the church at 9:45 A.M. for a service that began at 10:00 A.M., a routine I'd established in over a year of ministry at Connor's Corner. I walked into the choir room, expecting to find the choir robed and ready with their music and music folders—and there was no one there. I picked up a bulletin, which had been printed on the Friday before. To my amazement, where 'La Fiesta de la Posada' should have been listed, there was listed a hymn and the name of a soloist.

"I was stunned. I robed and raced out of the choir room in desperate search for a choir member and found Lydia, Robert's wife. Her face was a mask of concern.

" 'What is going on?' I blurted out. All she would say is: 'You'll have to talk to Robert about this.' I knew I couldn't press her. I finally found Robert and repeated my question, this time more demanding. Robert said sternly that it was entirely inappropriate for such a 'secular' piece of music to be performed in the worship service. Furthermore, he'd said he'd heard that I had been 'corrupting' the youth with 'secular songs.' Flabbergasted, I pressed for details, and Robert mentioned the song 'Let there be peace on earth' and told me angrily: 'It has no mention whatsoever of Jesus Christ.' He continued: 'We'll just have to talk sometime this week about your choice in music.'

"I was stunned and demanded to know why Robert or someone hadn't said anything about all this to me earlier in the week, even earlier in the fall. 'You must have known what we were rehearsing: we've been working on this piece for three months, and Lydia's in the choir!' Robert reminded me of our initial interview for the position. 'This is your own fault,' he told me. 'You caused this. I told you I had the final word in all matters concerning worship.'

"There was nothing more to be done: it was time for worship to begin. I led the singing, as I'd always done. I listened dispiritedly as a soloist wailed out special music when the adult choir should have been performing Brubeck, and during the sermon I wrote out my letter of resignation. I said that I wasn't resigning because my choice of music had been challenged. I was resigning because of the way in which that challenge had been issued. No one had spoken with me, and I could see that this was not a sudden decision: the bulletin had been printed on Friday. On Friday someone should have come directly to me about the change in plans. I concluded by stating that I would be willing to lead one more adult choir rehearsal, so that the choir would have some music to perform during the holiday. So after the service, I handed my resignation to Brother Robert, who read it and said without any affect: 'I accept your resignation. You can pick up the music in my office.' He did not suggest further conversation. This was the last time I would ever speak with him.

"I thought I might hear more information at the last choir rehearsal that Wednesday. But it seemed like people had changed overnight. They used the same kind of tone and language that Robert had. Several members accused me of being a 'liberal' for bringing such music into the church. Moreover, I had been 'corrupting' their youth with more 'secular' music. I was shocked with this sudden reversal from people with whom I had worked for a year. I hadn't heard anything like this expressed from the pulpit in the entire time I'd been at Connor's Corner. Moreover, since the congregation was fairly well-to-do, the same words would challenge some of the more comfortable life-styles of its wealthier members.

"I exploded in anger and gave an impassioned speech about how much external and material things mattered to these people: lyrics of songs, Christmas trees, symbols of Christmas. 'You are too concerned about outward appearances; you need to be a little more concerned about what's on the inside!' One of the members scoffed: 'You'd probably even like to go back to the Sixties with all the rest of those long-haired hippies!' I couldn't resist the challenge: 'I just might, because those long-haired hippies stood for peace and harmony, and I don't find much of that here!' But I knew the conversation was over when one of the deacons said: 'Well, I can see that we just don't have anything more to say to each other.'

"When I returned the scores, I told the whole story to some of the professors in the music department. By that time the sting of the whole event had worn off, and I was more baffled than anything else. I wondered if they might have any insight into the situation. All of them were pretty sympathetic, and one put his hand on my shoulder: 'Don't be upset. This kind of thing happens all the time.' Another was quite blunt: 'You'd better get used to this: it happens all the time in your line of work. You need to get used to this kind of treatment at the hands of preachers.'

"I never went back to Connor's Corner, nor did I ever contact any of its members again. In effect, I left never knowing exactly what had happened there or why the amazing reversal in attitude among its members. I needed some income and took another position immediately as a paid soloist in another church within the denomination where I could just walk in and walk out. A year later, I began attending a church in another denomination altogether."

"Power Over"

Kevin presented this case study in a course I taught, entitled "Power and Ministry." It was one of multiple case studies on power and abuses thereof that involved church organists or ministers of music. We noticed the recurring theme only when a student presented the final case study for the course. The case did *not* involve a church musician, and she titled it: "The Case of the Missing Church Musician." A volume on the important and often ill-defined role of church musician in the life of the church would probably be quite successful![1] But more seriously, all of the case studies that had coincidentally collected around the figure of the church musician involved dynamics of a kind of power I want to call "power over."

A few years ago, John Kenneth Galbraith observed that "few words are used so frequently with so little seeming need to reflect on their meaning as power."[2] Galbraith would be hard pressed to say the same today. Power has been a persistent topic of conversation in conferences of theologians and anthropologists, sociologists and political philosophers, and among groups that fall into categories of both "the powerful" and "the powerless."[3] There could even be a lively discussion between Lord Acton and psychoanalyst Rollo May over whether it is *power* that corrupts or *powerlessness!*[4] Yet beneath these various and diverse discussions and debates are facile dichotomies of powerful and powerless, of oppressor and oppressed.

Traditional discussions of power have been conducted from this point of vantage, with the resultant understanding of power as coercion, control, or domination. Defined this way, power is the ability to influence the behavior of others, and it is gained and exercised by tradition, force, consent, law, or authority. Examples come easily to mind. "Power over" is the traditional attitude toward nature, seen to be sanctioned by Scripture[5] and used to justify an instrumental approach to the environment.[6] "Power over" is the legal means at the hands of a minority South African government to enforce racial segregation on an entire people. "Power over" is the military coercion exercised by the Iraqi government over the Kurds, the commercial exploitation of African slaves in the seventeenth and eighteenth centuries, the ideological cult of terror practiced by conquistadors on the indigenous peoples in the Americas.

But there are other examples of "power over," which may come less easily to mind, because they are more pervasive. "Power over" rationalizes the traditional deference rendered by children to parents and adults. On one hand, such respect can protect children from experienced dangers; on the other, it can make them easy prey to adults and parents who would abuse or molest them. "Power over" is the traditional domination of husbands over their wives and children assumed in all too many marriages and buttressed by certain interpretations of Scripture and certain versions of political philosophy.[7] "Power over" is embodied in grades and inscribed on report cards. A teacher has the power to classify one student as "gifted," and place her in an accelerated program, and another as "exceptional," and place her in a program for "slow learners." "Power over" can refer to the seating arrangement at a banquet, the order of speakers on a program, the kind and length of coverage given news events from Latin America, Africa, and Europe on the evening news or on the front page of the morning paper. "Power over" is a fact of our quotidian world, all the more powerful when it is overlooked. Insofar as it goes unquestioned, unexamined, and unchallenged, insofar as it assumes absolute domination and totalitarian rule, "power over" is a form of power that is oppressive.

Abuses of "Power Over"

The dominant definition of power as "power over" has provoked three sorts of responses:

1. An outright refusal to discuss the subject at all. In decrying these various and nefarious expressions of "power over" as domination, coercion, and force, many leaders, particularly those who have experienced directly the abuses of "power over," refuse to talk about power at all. Lord Acton may have observed that "power corrupts," but here it is as if any discussion of power in any form also corrupts. Power is regarded as a mania of the dominant group, whether that group be "white people" or "men" or "patriarchy" or "the bourgeoisie." As a matter of principle, many minority groups tacitly agree neither to exercise nor to analyze power. For example, Nancy Hartsock notes this tendency among many women associated with the feminist movement and urges caution: "There is, after all, a certain dangerous irony in the fact that both feminists and antifeminists agree that the exercise of power is a masculine activity and preoccupation, inappropriate to women or feminists, and not a subject to which attention should be directed."[8]

2. A dismissal of "power over" as illegitimate in all of its manifestations, but willingness to identify other forms of power which may not be oppressive. Other leaders, again, particularly those coming from groups which have traditionally experienced the abuses of power, regard "power over" as an entirely illegitimate use of power, but attempt to articulate other kinds of power that might be less oppressive

and even empowering. Starhawk's assessment states eloquently this dismissal of "power over":

> Power-over comes from the consciousness I have termed estrangement: the view of the world as made up of atomized, nonliving parts, mechanically interacting, valued not for what they inherently are but only in relation to some outside standard. . . . We live embedded in systems of power-over and are indoctrinated into them, often from birth. In its clearest form, power-over is the power of the prison guard, of the gun, power that is ultimately backed by force. Power-over enables one individual or group to make the decisions that affect others, and to enforce control.[9]

In her constructive proposal, Starhawk moves to discover, delineate, and ritualize two other kinds of power, which she regards as more life-enhancing: "power-within" and "power-with."

Political philosopher Nancy Hartsock comes to a similar conclusion. Hartsock acknowledges that there might be *many* theories of power; in fact, she argues that there are as many theories of power as there are different kinds of community. She focuses on those definitions of power that have presented power as domination: economically as commodity and sexually as a violently expressed eros. But she moves beyond these definitions to suggest other definitions of power that might be more liberatory and that present power, not as domination or "power over," but as capacity or "power to."[10]

3. An acknowledgment of other forms of power, an openness to considering the possibility that even "power over" may have some place in the human community. Finally, other leaders call for a reassessment of "power over" itself, suggesting that it is not in itself destructive. While "power over" has tremendous potential for abuse, it may also have some constructive role to play in our daily lives. We could look at parenting as an example. Drawing on the work of Jean Baker Miller and the Stone Center for Developmental Services and Studies at Wellesley College in Massachusetts, Carter Heyward argues: "Any unequal power relationship is intrinsically abusive if it does not contain seeds both of transformation into a fully mutual relationship and of

mutual openness to equality."[11] The statement represents an important attempt to reassess "power over" by examining its potential for either abuse or transformation. This approach defines a third way of regarding "power over": a neutral relationship with the possibility of positive and negative uses. This approach closely parallels the understanding of "power over" presented here.

It is right to question abuses of "power over," but that does not mean that this kind of power is itself corrupt. Critical appraisal of this form of power merely means that it can be misused. Further, critical appraisal of "power over" does not mean that we should embrace without scrutiny other forms of power, as Starhawk does. Other forms of power, like coactive and charismatic power, carry their potential abuses as well, dangers to be treated here in subsequent chapters. If we concede that "power over" is not in itself diabolical, then the question becomes: What positive uses might this form of power have?

Uses of "Power Over"

"Power over" seems to have important place in certain areas of our lives. It is the power parents exercise in caring for their children. Certainly, this power can be—and occasionally is—abused. But at its best, this kind of power functions to protect a helpless infant against danger and death. It functions to set boundaries and foster individuation in a child. It finally empowers an adolescent to move out into the path of adulthood herself. This is nothing less than power as "power over."

"Power over" is also an important form of pedagogy, delineating the positions of teacher and student, of sage and disciple, of master and apprentice. Certainly, it can be used to overwhelm or intimidate; it can be used to commodify and quantify knowledge itself. At its best, however, "power over" in the service of *paideia*, acknowledges both teacher and student, disciple and sage, master and apprentice as pilgrims on similar journeys, then discerns the particular path each takes on that journey. This is nothing less than power as "power over."

"Power over" characterizes a doctor-patient relationship, when a sick person seeks out healing from a professional. Certainly, this relationship can be problematic, when a doctor withholds information from a patient or mystifies the patient with technology. At its best, however, the doctor-patient relationship trades on the relative expertise of each. The patient knows the disease, because he lives with it. The doctor knows the science and technology of healing, because she has been trained in it. Not unlike the doctor-patient relationship is the relationship between shaman and patient in the rain forests of the lower Andes. The shaman takes a purgative drink that induces visions clarifying both disease and cure. But first the patient must speak, often at great length, about his life, his illness, his family. Michael Taussig writes of this negotiation of power "in the relationship between the shaman and the patient—between the figure who sees but will not talk of what he sees, and the one who talks, often beautifully, but cannot see. It is this that has to be worked through if one is to become a healer."[12]

"Power over" grounds many aspects of a pastor-parishioner relationship, when a troubled parishioner relies on counsel and consolation from his pastor. This power is open to flagrant abuse, as an emerging literature on clergy sexual abuse amply documents.[13] But at its best, this form of power can help open the conduits for spiritual healing in both pastor and parishioner. This is nothing less than power as "power over."

Not all pastors want the power that is often vested in them by their churches. In particular, as positions of power in the lay and ordained ministries open to people who have traditionally been excluded from such posts, I often see these new leaders ready to exercise their power in every manner *but* that which is vested in them. Specifically, many people who have traditionally been excluded from positions of leadership are loathe to use the authority of their office: It represents the kind of power that has kept them out. They prefer instead to rely on charismatic power, "power within," or coactive power, "power with."[14] But uncritical exercise of charismatic or coactive power fails to acknowledge that these other forms of power also have their demons.

In the case of the Music Minister and the Preacher, we see this illustrated poignantly. Kevin had, in fact, all three forms of power. He had "power over" in the authority vested in the office of minister of music. This authority was buttressed spatially by the architecture of the chancel: He had a position of equal visibility, place, and power alongside that of the preacher. Yet,

Kevin's authority, his "power over," was merely nominal and visual. There was no written job description. There was no written contract hiring him to the position, nor did he have contact with any governing body inside the church. His sole superior was the preacher, whose "word was final." Perhaps Kevin accepted this a little too readily. The pronouncement may be expected of a stern father, but is it appropriate to an associate in ministry? Kevin seemed to acquiesce too quickly to a father-son relationship with Robert, raising the question of his own need for a father in the situation and his own desire to be in relationship with a stern parent.

In addition to these dimensions of "power over," Kevin possessed significant charisma—"power within." He had a great deal of energy and enthusiasm for his work and a genuine love of the people with whom he ministered. He assumed that he was inspiring and attractive to the members in general and to the youth in particular. After all, he always had Sunday brunch invitations, he had been asked to take over all youth activities, and he presided over a youth choir that was flourishing.

Finally, Kevin worked with a certain "coactive power." He led the members of his choir through the intricacies of jazz harmonies and rhythms. He helped them discover that they could master a difficult piece of music. This would create a feeling of empowerment for anyone! Thus, Kevin possessed in fact all three forms of power: "power over" or the power of the office, "power within" or charismatic power, and "power with" or coactive power.

Yet, clearly the most problematic form of power for Kevin was the form of "power over." Because of his age and experience, Kevin was most comfortable exercising other forms of power, his charismatic power and his coactive power. He really did not demand that the authority of his office be clarified or acknowledged by anyone other than the pastor, and this proved to be a serious omission. Moreover, he may have vested Robert with the authority of a stern father, an authority Robert may neither have wanted nor have known how to exercise well. Finally, an issue "at large" is the ambiguous role of ministers of music in general. The response of Kevin's professors to his dilemma indicated that his was not an isolated example.[15]

It seems then that this form of power is not intrinsically maleficent; indeed, to deny its place in our most ordinary relationships would be to deny the real differences in status, authority, and position that organize the way we relate to one another. The questions to put to this form of power are questions of its use and its effects. In a parent-child relationship, is this kind of power used to protect and nurture or to abuse? In a teacher-student relationship, is this kind of power used to educate or to overwhelm? In a doctor-patient relationship, is this kind of power used to heal or to disempower? In a pastor-parishioner relationship, is this kind of power used to inspirit or to control? The danger of this form of power is always the possibility of oppression.

"Power Over": Sovereign, Parental, and Bureaucratic

"Power over" describes relationships among both institutions and people which issue in dominance or subjection. These relationships may be either sovereign, parental, or bureaucratic. Often, as in Kevin's case study, elements of all three relationships may exist simultaneously!

1) "Power Over": A Sovereign Relationship

Perhaps sovereignty is the most familiar construal of "power over." The extreme of "power over" exercised in this fashion is in a community of warriors. Here the community is one under siege, a community whose survival is dangerously threatened by outsiders or enemies. Only two options are apparent: Either they conquer us or we conquer them, and, of course, it is clear whom we want to be the victors.

Certainly this siege mentality permeates Kevin's congregation at Connor's Corner. The boundaries between church and world are clearly defined. What is in the world is labeled "secular," and it is to be avoided at all costs. The final verdict rendered (by whom? Robert? the congregation? the deacons?) was that Kevin had faithlessly confused the necessary difference between the two and trespassed into the world. The community's judgments only reiterated the sense that the church is an outpost of faith in a hostile world. Kevin was accused (again, by whom?) of "corruption," of teaching "liberal" music to the choirs, of singing "secular" songs in church. Victory (whose?) would come only by expulsion of such traitors. These are the dictates of a siege mentality.

Yet, lest we over-problematize the warrior mentality, it is important to note that the church has often been threatened with extinction by outside pressures and persecution. When this is the case, language of conquest and competition invariably enters the arena of discourse. The martyrologies of the early church provide exciting witness to "athletes" for Christ, ready to compete for victory and the "crown" of eternal life against wild beasts.[16] "The Passion of Perpetua and Felicitas" relates the story of a young noblewoman and her slave in North Africa. Perpetua renounces her father, her child, and her wealth for the faith and stands steadfast in the face of jail, torture, and wild animals. In a vision she becomes a male wrestler, with seconds about her, and competes with an Egyptian wrestler, who she later discovers is the devil. As a woman, she receives the crown of victory. From the vision, she knows that she will be steadfast even to death.[17] Perhaps members of the church at Connor's Corner (who?) saw their church under no less a threat. Certainly, Kevin felt that he was a martyr to the church's mores. His final meeting with the adult choir was nothing less than an encounter in the arena, and his description of the bloodletting bears marks of these ancient texts: a verbal contest, a declaration of faith, physical suffering, and social alienation.

The mood in a community under siege is one of eternal vigilance, if not outright war. As he looked back at his time at Connor's Corner, Kevin felt as if he had been under constant surveillance. A song he'd taught to the youth long ago was presented as evidence of his "liberal" and "secular" tendencies. There had been no outcry at the time—but someone had remembered the incident and filed it away (who?). On Kevin's final Sunday, he discovered that someone (again, who?) had confiscated all scores of the Brubeck piece. Someone had to know where he'd kept his music in order to take it.

In communities under siege, various values are developed and practiced. Strength, competition, and physical prowess are admired and cultivated. Bodily needs and desires are brushed aside, because the possibility of death is so real. The virtues emphasized are virtues that prepare one for battle: courage and valor. Finally, because the threat of death, corruption, or contamination is alive and imminent, some means of achieving immortality must be present, so that one's accomplishments, one's honor, may live on. This is promised in the manner of songs sung and poems composed.[18]

Probably a lot of the hymnals at Connor's Corner contained hymns celebrating this kind of warrior mentality. Certainly, it is not a foreign sensibility to some churches today, particularly those that operate under situations of extreme oppression or those that see a sharp division between church and world, between "sacred" and "secular," between Christ and culture.[19] Throughout history, Christian churches have periodically been under threat—real or perceived—and our denominational hymnals bear witness to this: "Rise up, O men of God . . . / her strength unequal to her task; rise up, and make her great." "Soldiers of the cross" are climbing Jacob's ladder. Luther's great Reformation hymn compares God to "a mighty fortress." Did he have in mind the fortress at Wartburg, where he hid from Emperor Charles V?

Military language often occurs in a church under siege. But these warrior hymns have neither the lyrics nor the pacing of hymns like "Spirit of God, Descend upon My Heart" or "Breathe on Me, Breath of God," which witness to a spirit of charismatic power, or "What a Friend We Have in Jesus," which reflects more the coactive power of friendship. Perhaps no one has ever looked at the political theology of our hymnals, but it is there. As I've tried to illustrate, each hymn comes from a particular kind of community and addresses a particular kind of God. Communities are invariably, both overtly and covertly, arguments for certain relationships of power. Maybe we ought to pay more attention to what we sing!

A community of warriors expresses an extreme of sovereignty, the sovereignty that exists in conditions of siege. More mundane examples of sovereignty exist in ordinary political and communal relationships between a leader and the group being led. At first glance, one can demarcate clearly who is superordinate and who is subordinate. But is not the relationship more complex? Can a leader lead without consent of the governed? A group that refuses to follow has the ability to render the designated irrelevant.

What if Kevin had ignored Robert's leadership? or vice versa? What if the entire congregation had ceased to respect Robert's leadership? Whom would he then lead? Look at what happened when the congregation ceased to respect Kevin's leadership: He had to leave. These questions point to a powerful reciprocity between the leader and the group. Hannah Arendt's comments are worth quoting again in this context:

> Power corresponds to the human ability not just to act but to act in concert. Power is never the property of an individual; it belongs to a

group and remains in existence so long as the group keeps together. When we say of somebody that he is "in power" we actually refer to his being empowered by a certain number of people to act in their name. The moment the group, from which the power originated to begin with (*potestas in populo*, without a people or group there is no power), disappears, "his power" also vanishes.[20]

For Arendt power describes a relationship between a leader and a group, but one in which not dominance but empowerment characterizes the exchange between the two parties. In fact, the leader is empowered to lead the group. Should the group take away the empowerment, the leader can no longer lead.

The only option a leader without a group has is to revert to tyranny. Where consent of the governed is absent, the leader must rule by violence, force, or coercion. The tyrant articulates control by isolation, separation of subjects one from another, so that they cannot come together and create power.[21]

Arendt's analysis affords interesting comment on the case at hand. We do not know what really happened: We know neither who registered the complaint against Kevin nor how this was done. But we do know that Kevin no longer had any power to lead, because all empowerment from the congregation had vanished. He simply could not have continued his ministry at Connor's Corner. How this support vanished is even more of a mystery, but it is entirely possible that some tyrannical force isolated Kevin from the rest of the congregation. He came to represent the dangerous world outside the church, a representation fueled by all the suspicion and paranoia that accompanies tyrannies. His power vanished with his congregational support.

Whether it operates in warrior or tyrant modes, whether it operates more benignly with a leader acting with consent and cooperation of the governed, sovereignty is a prevalent means of exercising "power over" in congregational settings. But it is not the only means of exercising "power over."

2) "Power Over": A Parental Relationship

There is a second and emerging model of discussing "power over": a parental model. The model is discussed by some feminists as an alternative to "power over" as sovereignty.[22] A parental model has been equally criticized for essentializing women's experience, romanticizing motherhood and parenthood, and emphasizing caring and nurture as a resultant ethic.[23] Parenthood appears to be as problematic as was sovereignty as a way of analyzing "power over." Yet, its dimensions are present in the case under study, and its effects, both positive and negative, are evident in our own daily encounters with power. Understanding "power over" as sovereignty focuses on the voluntary or involuntary consent of the governed. Understanding "power over" as parenthood focuses on the issues of equality and inequality. To the degree that "power over" articulates a relationship of dominance, one person or group over another, it also delineates a relationship in which there is inequality of status, position, authority, or experience. This inequality is poignantly presented in a parent-child relationship.

The parent-child dynamic pervades the case under study. On the most obvious level, Kevin is initially given charge of the children's and youth choirs, and eventually he is asked to oversee the entire youth program. He is, then, the surrogate "parent" for these young children, a task he enjoys. In contrast to his colleague, Robert, who plainly confides that he didn't "get along" with children, Kevin does—and does so with evident success. Yet, there is another parent-child dynamic going on as well. Robert reminds Kevin of his own father, and the various eddies and currents of that relationship inform their ministry. Kevin seems comfortable with the distance between them, even as he admits that he wanted "a little more support" from Robert.

But Kevin's construal of their relationship may have created problems. He initially accepts Robert's statement that his "word is final" in matters of worship, neither challenging it nor investigating it, unlike a peer or an adult, who might have. Later, he seems to accept the judgment, and he leaves the congregation as an unjustly punished child. Even today, as he speaks of this experience long past, what seems to drive his words are the feelings of an abused child.

There is always the potential for abuse in a parent-child relationship; there is always the danger of dysfunction in a family system. The specter of each raises the issues of equality and inequality between parent and child. It is the inherent inequality between parent and child that is most volatile in any family relationship, biological or constructed. How parent and child deal with inequality opens the possibility for either abuse and dysfunction or empowerment. Recognizing this, psychologist Jean Baker Miller and theologian Carter Heyward suggest three criteria for distinguishing between these very different outcomes of this exercise of power.[24] Each hinges on the notion of equality.

1. The first criterion is that the relationship of inequality be temporary in duration, not terminal. This criterion is difficult to apply in Kevin's situation, because he was a college student who was hired for presumably interim work as a minister of music. But, certainly the meetings he requested with Robert could have been used as opportunities for important mentoring and preparation for Kevin's future in ministry. Unfortunately, those meetings were never made routine.

2. The second criterion demands that, despite any inherent external inequalities between the two parties, mutuality be a goal of the relationship. In other words, despite the fact that the two do not hold the same degree of power, the two parties need to be committed to a shared vision, toward which each is working.[25] In a sense and perhaps naively, Kevin assumed this mutuality in ministry: "I assumed that anything short of direct conflict constituted a good working relationship." Kevin's assumption was, however, never explicitly confirmed by either Robert or the board of deacons. When mission and collegiality are assumed and undiscussed, the questions "whose mission?" and "which understanding of collegiality?" are always masked. It suddenly became clear that Kevin's vision was not shared. Unfortunately, at the point at which the singularity of his vision became clear, there was no longer room for conversation. The words of the deacon from the final rehearsal are resonant: "Well, I can see that we just don't have anything more to say to each other."

3. Finally, a third criterion insists that both parties be able to envision a time in which equality would be present between them.[26] Probably part of the problem at Connor's Corner was confusion on the whole issue of equality. The configuration of worship space presented both preacher and minister of music as equals: Both occupied positions of equal stature on Sundays. Both were raised above the congregations by several steps; one sat at the right; the other, at the left. Perhaps this visual equality made it necessary for Robert to state firmly his superiority in precisely that setting in which it appeared to be equal to Kevin's: the arena of worship. The apparent equality did not extend into

the politics of congregational life. Robert's word, this time an affirmative one, had been final in terms of Kevin's appointment. He accepted, apparently without counsel with or challenge from the board of deacons, Kevin's resignation. A visual equality did not confer political equality.

The inequality between Robert and Kevin is common in familial networks. Ideally, these communities operate as organic wholes, with each part contributing its part to the functioning of the whole. Certainly, ministry appeared to be functioning quite well at Connor's Corner, with Kevin attending to the youth and the music and Robert attending to the deacons and the elderly. Robert had more contact with the people who had more power, and this buttressed the structural inequality between them. But, before things came to a head, each managed to minister both effectively and well in each of these spheres, using very different leadership styles. It seemed like a functioning and relatively healthy family.

Yet, appearances can deceive. Lest the parental model be perceived as unproblematic, the rest of the story illustrates well its problems. If the dangers of exercising "power over" as sovereignty are tyranny and domination, the danger of exercising "power over" in its parental mode is dysfunction. Dysfunction occurs when one part is not functioning as it should, and others move in to cover and to pick up the pieces. When a parent is disabled by mental illness or addiction or simple absence, children move in to do the parenting. A woman described jokingly her childhood: "The only vacancy left in my family was for an adult, so that's what I've been." At four years old, she turned forty. Usually, the vacancies are never advertised and never made public. Everyone simply pretends that this is what "normal" is like, until the pretense becomes the truth. Three commandments govern dysfunctional family life: Thou shalt not talk; thou shalt not trust; thou shalt not feel. No one ever acknowledges these exist; no one ever disobeys.

The dysfunctions at Connor's Corner became evident with the Brubeck composition. No one told Kevin what had happened, and he never investigated the circumstances. It could be said that he was in complicity in keeping the secrets. The complete reversal in people's bearing toward Kevin suggests that secrecy and rage were easier than trying to assess truth or falsity of the charges, than trying to trace down the possible motives of the accuser or accusers. The secrets still remain; the scapegoat was exorcised; the family was secure.

The problems and possibilities of "power over" exercised as parenthood are painfully apparent in this case study. An alternative to "power over" exercised as sovereignty, parenthood does not appear to be one that is any less problematic, but it is both different and appropriate in its place. Certainly, dimensions of a parental exercise of "power over" surface in the case under study. Yet, there is another exercise of power present as well: "power over" as bureaucratic power.

3) "Power Over": A Bureaucratic Relationship

Complicating the situation at Connor's Corner is the presence of bureaucratic power. It is present precisely because it is invisible. Evidence of this power has been parenthetically present throughout the foregoing discussion of "power over" as sovereignty and parenthood: "which?" "whose?" "for whom?" "by whom?" and finally, "who?" The answers to these questions are left open; the persons or structures to whom they point are masked. That very absence points to bureaucratic power, a power operative in the situation that is impersonal, constant, and anonymous.[27]

The superordinate-subordinate relationship between Robert and Kevin is buttressed by bureaucracy. It engages questions of authority, or bureaucratically sanctioned power. Authority is legitimate power; it connects power and legitimacy. Authority has often been defined as "belief in legitimacy, measured by voluntary compliance."[28] In the preceding chapter, we discussed the power that circulates as authority: It is external, public, and institutional. Certainly, each of these adjectives describes the power that both Robert and Kevin possess. Apart from who each is as a person, both have a designated role in the church, which is publicly acknowledged and spatially prominent. When Kevin joined the staff, he was introduced to the congregation as "Brother Kevin, our new minister of music." In themselves, the words are unremarkable, but they remind people of the external, public, and institutional character of Kevin's work. Kevin has authority.

But both men use their power and authority differently. For better and for worse, Kevin chose not to rely on the authority of his office, but to exercise his charismatic and coactive power instead. In contrast, Robert was a man who masterfully exercised the authority of his office. Characteristic of many possessing this kind of authority, a combination of what Max Weber would define as bureaucratic and traditional authority, Robert was a fairly impersonal leader. He showed little affect upon receiving Kevin's resignation, demonstrated little or no enthusiasm for his ministry at Connor's Corner, and in general, could barely be accused of being an "effusive" person. Authority works impersonally, emphasizing the office, not the person. There is much popular disdain for this kind of authority and the people who exercise it. Bureaucratic authority is challenged by many people who, like Kevin, don't need it, and "bureaucrats" are disregarded as feelingless, impersonal robots. They wear the masks. Richard Sennett identifies a bureaucratic prose style, which masks the one who is writing or speaking. A bureaucratic memorandum that begins: "It has been decided . . ." short-circuits the question, "Who decided this?" It's quite different to begin the same memorandum with the words, "The president of the church council has decided . . .," attaching a person to the decision. It's quite different for the author to speak, first-person singular: "I have decided."[29] These alternative forms of address counter a bureaucratic tendency to mask the speaker. But a bureaucratic form of address also masks the one spoken or written to: She is never addressed at all, much less addressed as "you."

There is significant masking in the case under study. Kevin never really found out what had happened. Who had brought these accusations of "corruption" against him? Who had found his music "secular" and "liberal"? Where had these words come from? Robert? a deacon? a concerned parent? the board of deacons itself? a coalition of members in the congregation? The accusers are masked. Moreover, Kevin is in complicity with this kind of bureaucratic power because he resigns, refuses further investigation, and does not demand that the masks be dropped.

Yet, lest we dismiss impersonal leadership entirely and applaud only what is personal, it is important to acknowledge that impersonal authority also has its place. It enables a pastor to minister to someone whom she really does not like; it enables a parishioner to receive ministry from a pastor whom he does not really admire. It enabled two persons like Kevin and Robert to minister together at Connor's Corner and even, for a time, effectively, despite their differences.

Ministry as "Power Over"

Ministry exercised as "power over" has unique problems and possibilities, whether that power is exercised as sovereignty, parenthood, or bureaucracy. These are abundantly presented in the case under study. When the church or the community is under siege, real or imagined, a "we-they" mentality rules the day and the emphasis is on the distinctiveness, uniqueness, and particularity of the defending community. The exercise of power within that community will reflect the enormity of the threat it sees itself facing. The promise of this exercise of power is survival; the danger is oppression of the outsider and the nonconformist. When the church or the community is trying to function as an organic unit, a "parts-whole" mentality manifests itself. The emphasis is on harmony, flexibility, and individuation. The exercise of power within that community reflects the need and desire to be whole. The promise of this exercise of power is integrity; the danger is dysfunction. When the church or the community is trying to function as an institution, a bureaucracy manifests itself. The emphasis is on rationality, impersonality, and control. The exercise of power within that community reflects the need for structure. The promise of this exercise of power is organization and objectivity; the danger is subjection and anonymity. Perhaps each of these forms of "power over" has its place—and needs to have its place if the churches are to continue to survive and to thrive. But each has its dark side; domination, dysfunction, and subjection are stifling to the message of a living Word.

Images of God

As one looks at these three forms of "power over," it is clear that certain images of God form and inform a ministry of "power over." These images fall, accordingly, into two categories. God as Sovereign, Master, Lord, or Judge can be used to buttress both the sovereign and bureaucratic exercises of "power over," and images of God as Parent, whether Father or Mother, can be used to buttress the parental model of "power over." These images of God confront us with the inherent Otherness of God.

These images introduce us to a God who is sometimes hidden from view. The God whom Jesus addressed with revolutionary tenderness, "Abba," is the same God he would later curse from the cross: "My God, my God, why have you forsaken me?" (Mark 15:34). The God whom Jesus spoke to as "Father" is the same God he would charge with abandonment. The God whom the prophets addressed as "the Most High God" is the child born in Bethlehem, the God who became incarnate. Martin Luther tried to capture this dialectic in his language about God. He spoke about a God who is revealed *(deus revelatus)*; but he spoke with equal conviction about a God who is hidden *(deus absconditus)*. Luther was constantly confronted with this mystery of powers in God.

One senses the conjunction was all-powerful, but not at all comfortable. Centuries before, Augustine burned lampfuls of oil while toiling over an ancient question: Why did God save Jacob and not Esau? He attempted first to speak of a "hidden merit" in Jacob, then a "merit of faith," then abandoned the attempt to find any answer in any difference between the two brothers. The difference lay in God, and he concluded with the words of Paul from his letter to the Romans: "O the depth of the riches and wisdom and knowledge of God! How unsearchable are his judgments and how inscrutable his ways!"[30]

The difference which puzzled Augustine and the mystery which awed Luther challenge easy images of God as Sovereign, Father or Mother, Judge or Lord. We see instead a Sovereign who empties God's power into humanity; a Parent who does not control, but rather suffers; a Leader whose face we may sometimes see—and sometimes not see. These images simultaneously challenge those who would seek easy theological justification of "power over."

First, God does not hoard power; God pours it out. This is presented in the kenotic Christology of Philippians 2:5-11. *Kenosis* means literally a "pouring out." God is Sovereign, Master, Lord, Judge who empties God's Self to become a human one, a servant, a slave, one who is judged. This kenotic characteristic is typical of the "power over" that God exercises. This is the curb against the threat of domination inherent in the warrior's, the tyrant's, or the bureaucrat's exercise of "power over."

Second, God does not hoard power, God pours it out—and God pours it out on us. Perhaps the closest word currently in vogue to describe this is "empowerment," but empowerment does not quite capture the meaning. Receiving God's power both empowers and requires. Not only does it enable us to reach our full humanity, but it carries with it a requirement. The requirement is crucial—and easily ignored. Through God's kenotic activity, we do not become God or gods or goddesses. It in no way diminishes or detracts from God; it merely enables and requires us to do nothing less than be disciples—and to exercise that power of discipleship in the way that we have been shown. This is the curb against domination, dysfunction, and subjection in the exercise of "power over."

Third, God suffers. This is nowhere more evident than on the cross. There is no attempt to manipulate or control events, so that things might have turned out a little less messy. God shows that God is able to withstand a mess not of God's own creation—but absolutely incapable of taking it without compassion. God shows compassion by literally "suffering with." This is the curb against dysfunction and a challenge to impersonality.

Images of Community

The subsequent challenge to us is clear: We too are enjoined to exercise a power that is consonant with this kind of God. Those who exercise power over others must be ever ready to pour it out upon them; those who exercise power over others must be prepared themselves to suffer. Understanding this mystery in God guides us toward ways in which "power over" can be used without the abuses of domination, dysfunction, or subjection.

What would a community that worshiped God as Sovereign, Master, Lord, and Judge look like? that worshiped God as Parent, whether Father or Mother? Sovereign and bureaucratic images of God engender a community that is counseled toward obedience and order and cautioned against disobedience and disorder. Parental images of God engender a community that is counseled toward honor and cautioned against dishonor.

Images of Leadership

A leader operating in this kind of "power over" mode would be acutely aware of the expertise provided by her training to engage in ministry and to equip others to do so. Awareness of this kind of power separates the leader from the group and the ordained minister from the congregation; it forces the leader to deal with differences, differences which are really inherent in the office. To pretend away such differences would be an act of denial. The strength of a "power over" model of ministry is to present honestly differences that really *do* exist between leader and group, as well as to emphasize a leader's responsibility to guide, nurture, and, when necessary, discipline the group or individuals therein.

At the same time, too much traffic with this "power over" mode feeds four unhelpful caricatures of ministry. The first caricature calls to mind the military model of exercising power in a congregation: the portrait of the *Herr Pastor* or *Frau Pastorin*. Here a leader exercises absolute and blind power over a group. This caricature points to the danger of absolutism, domination, and oppression inherent in a "power over" model of leadership. The second caricature calls to mind the parental model of exercising power in a congregation: the portrait of the Pastor as Eternal Earth Mother or Benign Father, a parent encouraging childlike and even childish behavior in a group through long-suffering patience. This caricature points to the danger of infantilization in the "power over" model of leadership. A third caricature, again from the parental model of exercising power, is the portrait of the leader as Compulsive Co-dependent, dangerously out-of-touch with her own feelings, but desperately sensitive to the feelings of the group and both anxious and able to control them. The co-dependent leader is unable to provide coherent and prophetic leadership and only encourages continuing dependence of the group upon its leader. This kind of leadership aborts all possibilities for growth, empowerment, and independence in the group. The caricature points to the lure of control and the seduction of indispensability lurking within the "power over" model of leadership. A final caricature is the Pastor as Manager, competent at organization and administration, but often locked away from the needs of the people through a complex network of technology and secretaries. Certainly, everything will run smoothly, but all creative chaos is stamped out before it has a chance to catch fire. Again, the lure of control fuels this, but unlike the Compulsive Co-dependent, here it is not cloying intimacy, but impersonal efficiency which characterizes congregational life. The caricatures point to problems with "power over" leadership, which must be held in tension with possibilities latent in its exercise.

Power II

Power Within
Discerning the Spirits

The Pastor and the Church Matriarch

"St. Paul's was a small working class congregation in a neighborhood that had a growing population of Asian-American immigrants. Its members had come out of a depressed Midwestern economy in the 1930s to work in the prospering shipyards—and stayed. Their children had been born, baptized, confirmed, and married in the church. Now, however, St. Paul's was an older congregation. The founding members were beginning to retire, and their children had all moved to outlying neighborhoods where jobs were more available. The congregation had adjusted to these changes by cultivating a close sense of community within and guarding its doors against changes from without. It had not engaged the surrounding community.

"Ruth had been one of the founding members of the congregation. Now in her mid-60s, her husband had died several years ago, and she filled her time with church activities. She volunteered several days in the church office, a job which, in a small congregation, she could pretty well define herself. She opened and sorted mail for the pastor, passing on those she deemed important and simply discarding everything else. Ruth also functioned as secretary to the church council. In that capacity she set the agenda and took minutes for all the meetings. She was president of the women's circle and convened the women regularly for coffee and Bible study. She had introduced a popular adult Bible study program in the congregation and initiated an excellent and still-functioning adult education program. She had spearheaded a movement to study the use of inclusive language in the liturgy. Ruth had even taken classes at the seminary, when I was a student there. She wanted to enhance her theological training, and she got along well with the rest of us students, unfazed by either our relative youth or our inexperience. I really liked her. She was articulate, confident, smartly dressed, and exuded a sense of *savoir faire*. She knew how the world worked.

"When the pastor at St. Paul's retired, I was put on the list of candidates for call to the congregation. I was 39 years old, fresh out of seminary, and had become familiar with the congregation during a field work placement there. Ruth was an enthusiastic supporter. She was on the call committee that interviewed me, and she was on the council that voted to call me. As the pastor prepared to leave, I recall a conversation with him. He offered a piece of advice, which perhaps was a warning: 'I regard Ruth as the pulse of the congregation.'

"As I began my ministry, I could see that Ruth was only too happy to function in this capacity. She had enjoyed a privileged relationship with the preceding pastor. She seemed to assume that the privilege would continue, only enhanced by the time we had spent in seminary classes together. I was frankly uncomfortable picking up that privileged relationship. It seemed to me dangerous as a new pastor to favor any one member of the congregation with special attention or tasks. In addition, I suspected that the previous pastor had flattered Ruth with an attention that I couldn't match. Anyway, I wanted to get a feel for the 'pulse' of the congregation myself. What was St. Paul's context and its potential for ministry in that context?

"I asked Ruth and the other woman who volunteered in the church office to continue opening the mail, but to pass all of it on to me for a few months, without sorting it. I asked Ruth, as secretary of the church council, to keep a file of all items that would merit the attention of the group. We would draw up the agenda from that file.

"I remember one conversation about the agenda file. It seemed insignificant at the time, and I can't even remember what the item was. But I had passed something on to Ruth for the next council meeting, and she skimmed it and handed it back to me: 'Well, Pastor, I just don't think they'll want to deal with this one.' I think I laughed, without realizing the significance of the exchange, and said lightly: 'Then, *they* can decide *they* don't want to deal with it.'

"The first direct conflict that I can recall surfaced over the issue of building use. Ruth had always received requests for building use in the mail, and she had passed on those she deemed 'worthy' to the council and simply discarded those requests she felt the council 'wouldn't want to deal with.' A request came to the church from a Laotian refugee project, Origins, which had been organized under the auspices of Catholic Charities. The group needed classroom space for offering English as a Second Language classes to the Laotians. Because so many of the refugees were former farmers, there was a perceived need to acquaint them with American means and tools of farming. The group had secured the help of a working farm nearby, but much of the acclimation involved classroom instruction. The group had been renting classroom facilities at another local church, but recently been told it had to move. A request for building use came to St. Paul's.

"I checked into the group's insurance and its non-profit organization status. I got a green light on all fronts, and I put the matter before the church council. The discussion at the council meeting was heated, and it quickly became apparent that Ruth, among others, was opposed to this group's use of the church building. This was not a request she would have forwarded on to the church council herself, had she still been responsible for sorting mail and had she still been solely in charge of setting the agenda for council meetings. The discussion turned into an argument between the two of us. Ruth argued, 'If the Roman Catholics brought them over here, *they* should take care of them. We shouldn't. It's *our* church and *our* country.' I countered: 'That's just not a valid argument. The church doesn't acknowledge political boundaries. If we have to say no, we should just say "No." We don't say "it's someone else's responsibility." ' "

"I sensed that the vote that night was influenced more by financial need than any sort of political theology. The council voted to let Origins use the church facilities—with a series of contingencies. I thought some of these were unnecessary, but they served to appease those councilmembers like Ruth who'd been overridden. Origins would use three upstairs rooms on the second floor that were currently vacant and had formerly been Sunday School rooms when the congregation's children had been younger. The group was to use the bathrooms at the base of the stairs, behind the stage in the fellowship hall. These had been the Sunday School facilities and were now never used by members.

The group was restricted to the back entrance of the church, also behind the stage. Only the three (Caucasian!) staffpersons were to have access to the fellowship hall through the front door of the church.

"Ruth's final protest that evening was to argue that the congregation didn't have the resources to clean the upstairs rooms and the bathrooms behind the stage, as well as its own sanctuary, fellowship hall, and the main toilet facilities. I was unwilling to concede what I considered a major step toward openness to the community. 'Look,' I suggested, 'We'll make it a condition of the lease that the group clean its own rooms and bathrooms.' With little further discussion and a strong sense of the needed income this lease would bring, the motion passed.

"Origins moved in. The group agreed to honor the contingencies on their lease, and offered to clean, not only their own rooms, but the entire church. The offer freed the church from the financial burden of a janitorial service; it was accepted immediately. But the presence of Origins at St. Paul's was punctuated by several incidents early in its lease. Respecting the restrictions on space, the Laotians ate lunch every day outside on the patio. Complaints began to trickle into my office: 'the patio is being wrecked!' I passed these on to the leaders at Origins. The group responded by volunteering to keep up not only the patio, but the whole of the church grounds! Again, the council accepted the offer, and the incident was defused.

"A second incident was harder to settle. A community-sponsored senior center used the fellowship hall, kitchen, and main bathroom every Thursday from mid-morning into the early afternoon, offering a hot meal at noon. When they passed the Laotian students in the parking lot, many of the seniors were rude to them. One Wednesday afternoon the cook for the senior center entered the kitchen to find a Laotian man there, 'barefoot and stripped to the waist!' as she later reported to me with some emotion. She was indignant, but not fearful. I pressed for details. He had been cleaning with his shirt off and startled her as she brought in groceries for the hot meal the following day. He was apologetic; she was angry and registered vigorous complaint with me, demanding that the matter be raised with the church council. I added the complaint to the file of items for the council agenda.

"The whole matter was addressed at the next council meeting. The initiating issue was the complaint filed by the cook, which was reported in detail, down to her stated description that the man had been 'stripped to the waist.' Throughout the report, there was a mounting tension in the room. Then, a male council member asked drily: 'From the waist up? or from the waist down?' I remember hearing a few nervous titters, and I tried to imagine what might have happened had one of the men on the council been in the kitchen, 'barefoot and stripped to the waist.' Then someone else added: 'Look: they've brought so much stuff here. Desks, chairs, files, books and bookcases—even the engine of a tractor! They're just taking the place over!' The collective image of a tractor engine spread carefully across a tarpaulin on the floor of what had been the second-grade Sunday School room drifted across everyone's mind.

"I braced myself and began to speak slowly and carefully: 'Let's think about this. Other groups using our facilities bring things into the church. The senior center has brought dishes and utensils, pots and pans, files and books and bookcases. And it isn't accused of taking the place over. When the seniors leave something out of place, we put it away ourselves, and we chalk up the extra effort to "ministry." But when Origins brings in its material, when Origins leaves something out of place, it's definitely *not* OK.' I paused for a breath, trying to assess the impact of my words: 'I wonder if anyone else has noticed the difference in the way we're relating to these two groups using our church?'

"The response to the question was immediate. It also seemed to me somewhat defensive. Someone responded: 'It's not *racism*, if that's what you're trying to imply—' I had in fact consciously avoided using the term. '—it's just that some of these other groups have been here longer.' Then, Ruth entered the discussion: 'Well, they can be here, but once they're in *this* country, and in *this* church, they should do things *our* way.' Her comment puzzled me: it seemed uncharacteristically inflexible. I responded: 'But what right do we have to say that *our* way is the *right* way?' Ruth shot back: 'Well, what right do *you* have to change the Bible?'

"I was stunned! The challenge took me by complete surprise. It took me a moment to realize that Ruth was referring to my efforts to use inclusive language in the liturgy, to pencil marks I had made in the pulpit Bible to indicate more inclusive pronouns for humanity than 'man' and 'men,' 'his' and 'him.' But now I was only more baffled. When I'd started the call at St. Paul's, the congregation had, by general consensus, agreed to use inclusive language in reference to humanity. What Ruth was challenging was that consensus, which I'd just assumed still held. Even more confusing, though, was that Ruth herself had been one of the first to initiate this movement toward inclusive language. Her objection at this point seemed to me out of the blue. I tried to choose my words carefully: 'The question of inclusive language in the liturgy and the question of Origins' use of our building space are two separate questions. I want to reserve discussion of the language issue for a later meeting. Now we have to talk about Origins.' I paused. I was not at all sure that these *were* two separate issues, and they certainly were the same issue for Ruth. But what was that issue? We needed to talk, and I needed to acknowledge that publicly: 'Ruth, it sounds like there's a lot of personal stuff that you and I need to talk about sometime.'

"That conversation was long in coming. The discussion about Origins at that council meeting ended with no particular resolution. In subsequent weeks, however, council members went out of their way to be friendly to the Laotian students, and other congregation members gradually followed suit. I put the inclusive language question in the file for items to be discussed at the next council meeting.

"At that council meeting Ruth took the lead by asking for a vote on inclusive language. I tried to intervene: 'This doesn't seem like something we should vote on. It's something we need to discuss and get consensus on, like we did before. To vote on this would be like voting on whether the late-coming laborers to the vineyard get a full day's wages or not!' There was some laughter, and again humor seemed to defuse the situation. Then, I added with more seriousness: 'I thought we had consensus on this matter, and clearly that has dissipated. We need to test that consensus.' In the ensuing discussion the council agreed to get bulletin inserts which had all the lessons printed out in inclusive language. As for the scripture readings during the service, we agreed that the lay readers could read from either the pulpit Bible (RSV) or the bulletin inserts, whichever was more comfortable to them. As for the liturgy itself, we agreed that inclusive language would only be used for humanity. The compromise seemed satisfactory.

"In subsequent weeks, I noticed that whenever Ruth read the lessons, she used the pulpit Bible exclusively. This continued to baffle me: Ruth had been an early supporter of inclusive language in the congregation, and I could find no explanation for her reversal. I did not question her about any of this. Indeed, I found it difficult to initiate the conversation I'd publicly said that we needed. We were able to get along cordially, if somewhat formally, and that seemed comfortable to both of us. In general, I could see Ruth was having to work harder to hold things together.

"About a year later Ruth announced plans to move to the Southwest to be nearer her family. Her absence would create a huge vacuum in the congregation's life: a new volunteer would be needed for the church office, a new secretary for the church council, a new coordinator for the adult Sunday School, a new president for the women's group. It was this last position that bothered Ruth the most. One Sunday during coffee hour, I noticed that all the women had gradually departed from the fellowship hall. I went into the church office, and they were gathered in the conference room. The door was closed. There was obviously a meeting in progress, but I had had no notice of a special meeting of the women of the congregation, a meeting to which I would have usually been invited.

"One of the other members of the group reported to me what had happened that Sunday. Ruth apparently began the meeting asking if anyone wanted to be president of the women's group. No one spoke up. She then announced that the women's group would disband, since no one wanted to be president. When I heard that I was shocked! The move would have been a singular embarrassment for me, as I was serving that year as synodical chaplain to the women's groups throughout the region. It would have been quite uncomfortable for my own church *not* to have had a chapter! The decision to disband seemed all but final, when one woman asked: 'But why do we need a president? Can't we still keep meeting and attending synodical functions without a president? We can figure out among ourselves how we want to be represented and who will do it.' The suggestion seemed so simple! It was easily seconded by women who'd enjoyed having coffee and reading the Bible together. The suggestion seemed to empower them to take action on their own and independently of Ruth. The women's group continued in existence; Ruth began to gather her things for the move.

"The farewell parties that preceded her departure were numerous, but I was invited to none of them. Some of the members were a little embarrassed about this, but I made light of it. Ruth's final Sunday at the church was the last week of my vacation. When I got back, I stopped by the house to say goodbye and to engage the conversation I myself had requested over a year ago. Ruth's car was not in the driveway, but I knocked anyway, preparing a card which would say the necessary words of farewell. To my surprise, Ruth came to the door.

"I initiated the conversation with words I'd rehearsed: 'I wanted to say goodbye and give us both some closure. We've had a lot of history together, and I certainly value you as a person. I have some grief that this part of our history has ended so badly. I also know that no amount of talking will probably get us past some of our differences. I have neither the skills nor the ability to offer you my reconciliation, but I want to claim the reconciliation of the Spirit of Christ for both of us.' To my surprise, Ruth reached out and embraced me. We chatted for a few minutes more, small talk, news of common acquaintances. Then I drove away, surprised by the warmth of Ruth's embrace.

"Six months later Origins left St. Paul's. The organization had found another facility that was more convenient to its working farm. The women's group continued, presidentless. About two years later I saw Ruth across a crowded room at a synodical convention. We greeted each other enthusiastically, and Ruth pressed me for news of her former congregation. It was as if we were still in seminary together, and nothing had happened."

"Power Over" and "Power Within"

The Pastor and the Church Matriarch is a story about racism and prejudice. It is a story about two women a generation apart in a church that has only recently opened its positions of ordained leadership to women. It is a story about the reconciliation of the Spirit of Christ. But it is also a story that poignantly illustrates a second form of power: "power within" or charismatic power.

This second form of power is similar to and yet quite different from the first form of power, "power over." A charismatic leader can inspire and empower; she can also dominate and oppress, a result of the exercise of "power over" that becomes tyranny. Ruth's charismatic power at St. Paul's illustrates all consequences. Her leadership was initially quite empowering, particularly her work with adult Bible study and the women's group. Then gradually it took on the edge of control. In sorting mail she maintained complete control over which communications and requests both the pastor and the church council would receive and entertain. In setting the agenda for the church council, she maintained control over items for council discussion and the order in which they were addressed. Finally, as her last act in the congregation before departing, she attempted to shut down the women's group, which presumably could not function in her absence. All these are instances of a charismatic power that works to dominate. Ironically, Ruth's leadership is finally ignored by the very people whom she helped empower. One of the women in the women's group asked a question which deflated completely her leadership: "But why do we need a president?"

Yet, charismatic power is very different from "power over" in terms of its legitimation. "Power over" is validated by external authority; "power within" is validated through the personal force of the one possessing it, literally the "charisms" or gifts of the leader. The source of Ruth's power was internal and personal. Her intelligence and articulateness, her unstinting hard work and *savoir faire:* All made her an indispensable member of the congregation.

But the authority for such leadership proved to be quite fragile. Generated by and within Ruth, it depended on a covert complicity with the group of people who recognized her as leader. Probably her authority was never explicitly acknowledged, aside from occasional comments like, "Well, we'll just send Ruth to represent us," or "Ruth would be a natural for that." Challenges to her leadership surfaced when Pastor Jane insisted on different ways of dealing with mail, agendas for the church council meetings, and building use. These changes in congregational procedure were initiated by someone who had a publicly designated leadership role in the congregation, a role Ruth herself had supported. Ruth was faced with a dilemma—either to back someone whose very *modus operandi* undermined the carefully constructed edifice of power she had built or to assert her traditional role. As we have seen, Ruth chose to reverse herself and challenge her pastor—and her pastor's power—directly. But Ruth's dilemma was not the only one. The congregation also was faced with a dilemma. Members were caught between supporting an old friend who had been a long-time leader to them and putting their weight behind their newly called pastor. Their discomfort was evident in the dance of affirmation and avoidance that accompanied Ruth's going away parties. Pastor Jane's comment is telling: "I could see Ruth was having to work harder to hold things together." If Ruth and the congregation couldn't continue their tacit agreement regarding her leadership, it would fall apart.

This stands in sharp contrast to the kind of power that Pastor Jane herself possessed: the power of an authority which was external, public, and institutional. Pastor Jane had been recommended to the congregation by synodical judicatories and elected as its pastor by majority vote of the congregation. Her authority was externally legitimated: by the synod and by the people of the congregation. She had been publicly installed with representatives from neighboring churches and synodical officials in attendance. Challenges to her leadership would have come from the very people who had chosen her, and challenging her leadership would have mandated that they examine their own judgment. Pastor Jane also possessed a great deal of charismatic power; that is, internal qualities that enhanced her external authority. Both she and Ruth were charismatic leaders. But Pastor Jane had the additional weight of externally legitimated power: the "power over" invested in her as a leader.

The genderedness of ecclesiastical configurations of power is particularly important and profoundly moving in this case. When Ruth was Pastor Jane's age, there were no externally legitimated places for women in leadership roles in the church. Women were not being ordained; the women who were presidents of church councils were few and far between. The roles for women in leadership positions were restricted to the positions of church secretary, Sunday school teacher, president of the church women's group, possibly Sunday school superintendent. This is not to suggest that women had no leadership positions in churches before women's ordination. But two observations are important. First, opportunities for externally legitimated positions of leadership were far fewer for women than for men. Second, any additional leadership women exerted was effected largely through the exercise of charismatic power, or "power within." Not surprisingly, women who have long been excluded from holding positions of externally legitimated power, like the positions of pastor or church council president, might well be suspicious of all those who do, even and especially when those people are women.

Ruth's reaction to Pastor Jane was probably shaped in part by the fact that she was relating to "Pastor" Jane, a woman holding a traditionally male role and exercising a traditionally male authority, which had long been used to block women from positions of leadership in the church. To the degree that the two women were competing for "inclusion" in a basically male-dominated ecclesiastical structure, each saw the other as a rival for the small amount of space open to women's leadership.

Authority is a means of legitimating power. It can be defined as power that is institutionalized, and the legitimation may be social convention or law or custom or tradition. The authority behind the parental form of "power over" is the weight of custom and the burden of tradition, buttressed in the West by law. The authority behind the warrior and bureaucratic forms of "power over" is the freight of law or the threat of violence or dismissal. But the legitimation in charismatic power is nothing more and nothing less than the personal magnetism of the leader herself. As such, "power within" is truly the fruit of a charism or gift; as such, it is the sum of one's spiritual, emotional, and psychological resources, and it legitimates itself. Ruth had these charisms in abundance: a bright and articulate person, she was skilled at getting things done and making people feel at ease. "Power within" is often spoken of as self-legitimating. It is its own authority, an internal authority or a personal authority.

Possibilities of "Power Within"

This form of power is creative and dynamic—often iconoclastic. It is quick to change and size up new opportunities, eager either to challenge old ways of being or to infuse them with new meaning. Ruth embraced the opportunity to educate herself theologically and took numerous classes at a nearby seminary. She saw the potential for a denominational Bible study program for her congregation; she had worked to implement it in the congregation; she had shaped it into a viable and dynamic adult education program. The creative program and education that Ruth brought to the congregation at St. Paul's were gifts that persisted long after her departure. These are the marks of a charismatic leader.

Because of its creativity and dynamism, charismatic power is inherently unstable. With no external grounding, it depends doubly upon the leader's ability to continue to impress and the people's willingness to continue to be impressed. After Pastor Jane's arrival, Ruth had to work harder to maintain her power base in the congregation. She had to work harder to continue to impress. Equally critical, her grasp on power depended on her peers' willingness to be impressed—which proved to be somewhat shaky. A member of her women's group punctured her power with a simple question: "But why do we need a president?" The group had decided it could get along without a president—and without Ruth. Had she passed on the charisms of leadership? lost them? or both?

Not surprisingly, and as we have seen, "power within" has often operated as a challenge or limit to "power over." In the early centuries of Christianity, the role of the prophets diminished as the role of bishops and teachers increased. In part, the issue was one of power: The charismatic power of prophets threatened emerging structures within the new church.[1] The charismatic power of prophets attracted people to a person; the institutional power of bishops and teachers gathered people into a community that was hunkering down for the long haul. Bishops and teachers embodied an institutional "power over," which was externally legitimated by ritual and apostolic succession. Gradually these institutional leaders reserved for themselves the right by emerging ecclesial law to decide who "true" and "false" prophets were, then finally edited out altogether those representatives of a power from within.

Centuries later, radical reformer Thomas Muentzer gathered around himself huge followings of peasants, disfranchised equally by a Roman Catholic emperor and by magisterial reformers, like Martin Luther, who had aligned himself with powerful princes. Muentzer was judged a threat by emperor and reformer alike. Muentzer claimed election by the Spirit both for himself and for the brave band of warriors who accompanied him. The Spirit—and not Christ, as the Lutherans would argue, nor tradition, as the Roman Catholics had held—would be the hermeneutic for unlocking the meaning of the Bible.[2]

Teresa of Avila was possessed of great charismatic power: She saw visions, herself was levitated off the floor in fits of spiritual ecstasy, heard voices. Moreover, she enjoyed the company of others, and her convent was full of visitors anxious to hear of her visions and desirous of modeling her life. Her charismatic power was held in check by a spiritual director, who monitored carefully her visions and her voices to be certain that they were of God and not Satan.[3] Eventually, Teresa was canonized, a move that both recognized her exceptional spiritual gifts and ensured that they would be regarded for posterity as "exceptional," that is, extra-ordinary. The history of the Christian churches is rife with stories of charismatic leaders and with the countermoves of an institution determined always to keep these stories subplots within the mainstream tradition.

There are myriad examples closer to home. The charismatic movement within the established churches during the sixties afforded people who were neither pastors nor priests their own access to power through speaking in tongues, healing, and ecstatic interpretations of the Bible. Again, a power from within directly threatened a "power over" exercised and authorized by institutions. The fate of the charismatic movement was twofold. In some instances, it died off entirely, no trace remaining. In other instances, however, the charismatic movement became institutionalized in the forms of regular healing or prayer services, which were scheduled outside the main worship service and attended by a small group of devotees or of communities practicing the gifts. Twentieth-century German sociologist Max Weber calls this phenomenon the "routinization of charisma" and regards it as an almost inevitable outcome of genuine charisma that seeks legitimation.[4]

Yet, charisma is precisely what establishes power in any group or person initially breaking into the mainstream. Institutional authority—or power conferred from above—is not immediately forthcoming; such a "power over" is more cautious, waiting on the sidelines to see who this person is, how she is, and how she is going to be received. A charismatic power, or "power within," must operate in individuals who break down barriers and open doors. Doubtless, it was the competence and charisma of people like Ruth that began to convince churches that women too should be ordained.

Abuses of "Power Within"

Ample examples, historical and modern, show how charismatic power operates in ways that are distinct from and even threatening to institutionalized forms of "power over." And yet, lest those in the counterinstitutional crowd among us get too excited, recall that "power within" runs its own obstacle course. Charismatic power is a gift that can poison; it needs constantly to be tested and tried. Jim Jones was such a charismatic leader, possessed perhaps more of his own demons than of any clear vision for his followers. They followed him blindly—even to their own deaths. Charismatic power is a prerequisite for television evangelists, and they preach at length with great power and efficacy, but also often with some overt or covert manipulation of their audiences. Ruth's charismatic power was sorely tested by her pastor's institutional authority; yet, she almost succeeded in shutting down a women's group in the wake of her departure. "Power within" ought to be disciplined and tested. At the same time, it is difficult to test—too often the bedazzled crowds will be too mesmerized to ask for authenticity. It appears that here, as with "power over," "power within" is another form of power that is literally ambivalent: It has the power to hypnotize and the power to liberate. Again, like "power over," charismatic power is not in itself dangerous, but it can certainly be used in various and nefarious ways. How are we to understand this power and its use?

Uses of "Power Within"

Charismatic power is affiliated in the Bible with blessings and curses. Not just anyone was able to hail a curse down upon the enemy or to shower a blessing upon a friend: Only those with recognized internal power or psychic energy could do so. Blessings and curses could not be delivered by just any worshiper. This kind of power legitimated a charismatic individual or shaman. Balaam from the book of Numbers appears to be just such a shaman, a combination of prophet and medicine man. Balak, king of the Moabites, saw the people of Israel camped out on the plains of Moab, and he got frightened. He summoned Balaam, the resident shaman and distributor of blessings and curses, and commanded him: "A people has come out of Egypt; they have spread over the face of the earth, and they have settled next to me. Come now, curse this people for me, since they are stronger than I; perhaps I shall be able to defeat them and drive them from the land; for I know that whomever you bless is blessed, and whomever you curse is cursed" (Num. 22:5-6). The request of the king places confidence in the shaman's power to bless and curse.

Of course, the story goes on, and Balaam's power to bless and curse is revealed to be not his power alone. It is not Balaam the shaman, but an unnamed ass, who sees the angel. For his visions, the ass at first receives only beatings. Then, "A speechless donkey spoke with a human voice and restrained the prophet's madness" (2 Pet. 2:16). It is the ass who places Balaam in contact with the source of all blessings and curses. Chastened, Balaam returns to Balak, king of the Moabites, and says: "How can I curse whom God has not cursed? / How can I denounce those whom the Lord has not denounced?" (Num. 23:8).

The story is fascinating, but particularly as a story about charismatic power. The unique power of the shaman to bless and curse is quite different from the power at the hands of his king. And the king knows it! Balak, with his armies and soldiers, possesses power as a warrior, but it is power to coerce. That power of coercion alone will not be efficacious in this situation, and Balak senses failure. He is driven to seek from a shaman who rides on an ass a kind of power that he, with all of his horses and all of his men, does not possess. The king seeks an additional power that has more to do with inspiration and inspiriting, with hope and creativity. Balak had the physical strength at his disposal. The king needed spiritual sustenance, something he thought only the shaman could summon.

Unfortunately, Balak should have been talking to Balaam's ass. The ass saw the source of all blessing and cursing. Connecting with that vision, Balaam could only report to Balak that he could not act in a way contrary to the One who was the source of all his power. Living with a keen sense of the supernatural and the realm of spirits distinguishes between a kind of "power over," the province of kings and commanders, and a kind of "power within," the province of priests and shamans. Michael Taussig points to the resistance embedded in shamanistic practices in the Putumayo forests of southwestern Colombia. Healing diseases and undoing sorceries of jealous neighbors, the shaman opens the space of death as a space of healing. The disjunction created between the power relations established in centuries of colonialism and those created in practices of shamanic healing opens a new space for negotiation between the colonizers and the colonized. The colonizers come to a native healer.[5]

Dorothy Emmet similarly contrasts the power of kings and the power of priests. Investigating various Greek and Latin words for "power," she notes that the Greek word *menos* denotes access to an energy which the gods may communicate to a person like Balaam, an animal like Balaam's ass, or a plant like the vision-inducing plant used by Taussig's shamans in the Putumayo forests, yagé. The connotation of both the Greek *arete* and the Latin *virtus*, both words for excellence, signified an inner power that could pass from person or plant or animal. She notes that Saul's power to reign, granted him by YHWH and expressed in the Hebrew word *kabod*, passes dramatically from him and onto David: "Now the spirit of the Lord departed from Saul, and an evil spirit from the Lord tormented him" (1 Sam. 16:14). "And then," Emmet writes, "the cry is *'Ichabod'*—'the glory has departed.' "[6]

Other words in other languages bear this sense of "power within." Emmet notes that they are all quite different from notions of "power over," the predominant connotation of power for modern culture. For her, the burden of this linguistic evidence from other cultures suggests that we need to expand our notion of power, which she finds to be largely restricted to domination and control—"power over" as sovereignty or tyranny—to include some evidence of "power within," or charismatic power. When we think, then, of what kind of power this charismatic power is, Emmet's discussion suggests that it is internal, often ecstatic, personal, that it is or mediates a divine or spiritual power. Where "power over" is often regarded as a kind of possession, "power within" is more a capacity or "power to."[7]

The Charismatic Leader

But what of the people who possess this kind of power? Max Weber has sketched the classical portrait of the charismatic leader in his essay "The Sociology of Charismatic Authority."[8] Here he contrasts charismatic with patriarchal and bureaucratic types of authority. Patriarchal or traditional authority depends on status relations, understood and accepted within a community, without requiring legal definition. This is similar to the parental kind of "power over." Bureaucratic authority is more a functional authority, requiring recognized and recognizable roles and rules. This is similar to the warrior mode of "power over." In contrast to these two kinds of patriarchal or bureaucratic power, a charismatic leader inspires allegiance through personal magnetism. Weber notes that founders of religions are usually charismatic leaders—but adds that a pirate chief may well possess charismatic qualities: "Pure charisma does not know any 'legitimacy' other than that flowing from personal strength, that is, one which is constantly being proved."[9] It inspires in its followers "a devotion born of distress and enthusiasm."

Weber addresses the various characteristics of charismatic leadership in a manner that is helpful and has been taken by the tradition of sociologists following him as normative. Drawing on his analysis, Raymond Trevor Bradley isolates eight characteristics of charismatic leadership. These illumine the story of Ruth and Pastor Jane.[10]

1. There is minimal delegation of power. The charismatic leader is the sole possessor of the goods and maintains these under his control at all times. As we have seen, Ruth maintained complete control over mail and the agenda for the church council. Rather than delegating these tasks either to the pastor or to the church council, she made peremptory decisions about what would be discussed and what requests she would pass on to the church council. Pastor Jane's attempt to delegate authority to the church council broke this control.

2. Each follower is directly accountable to the leader; there is a direct, personalized relationship of authority between the leader

and each follower. The personalization of this bond between leader and follower casts the relationship between them less in terms of duty and obligation, more in terms of affection and loyalty. The congregation was literally caught in a cross-fire between duty to their pastor and loyalty to Ruth. Hence, all the going away parties for Ruth carefully avoided this conflict: The pastor was simply not invited.

3. The leader holds complete control over the allocation of positions. Ruth's control over allocation of positions is nowhere clearer than in her attempt to abolish the presidency of the women's group and, in effect, the women's group altogether. Interestingly, the evidence that her charismatic power had diminished was indicated by a single question: "But why do we need a president?"

4. Basic needs will be met by a communal, subsistence economy based on gifts, booty, and so forth, involving few economic activities. Ruth's power consisted largely of her indispensability to the retiring pastor and in favors and kindnesses rendered—and remembered!—to various other members of the congregation.

5. There is a minimal amount of hierarchy: the leader, the disciples, and the followers. This point prescinds from the first point: In a system in which there is very little delegation of power, the hierarchy simplifies. Before Pastor Jane came, Ruth even had charge of the pastor. After all, he depended on her for the "pulse of the congregation." Pastor Jane entered with a demand that the congregation take its own pulse, identify its own ministry needs, and figure out ways to meet them.

6. There are no formal rules, institutions, or legal-judicial procedures. All decisions are made by the leader on an individual basis by decrees. Ruth attempted several times to issue decrees: deciding to disband the women's group and calling for a vote on inclusive language in the church council meeting. These she simply mandated of the people meeting with her. Interestingly, it was the invocation of precedent and of institutional rules and procedures that countered her decrees. In the situation involving Ruth's request for a council vote, Pastor Jane deferred to the congregational precedent on inclusive language, wherein the congregation engaged in education and discussion and came

finally to some consensus on the issue. In the situation involving the women's group, one woman simply stated that the group didn't procedurally need nor was it juridically required to have a president in order to belong to the denominational chapter of women's circles. In each situation, externally legitimated authority was summoned to counter the internal authority of a charismatic leader.

7. The whole structure can be changed by a decree from the leader. Again, this is clear from Ruth's attempts to edit out of congregational life its women's circle. Indeed, she even attempted to eliminate changes she herself had established. An early advocate of inclusive language, she reversed her position completely—and suggested that others do the same.

8. Charismatic leadership is a temporary and unstable phenomenon, always contingent on the leader's ability to prove his or her charismatic powers to the followers. To become a stable and permanent relationship, charismatic leadership must undergo routinization to become a tradition or rational authority structure, or a combination of both. Ruth sensed the fragility of her leadership base and, when it was threatened, worked hard to secure it. Had she become a "tradition" at St. Paul's? Certainly, her followers did not question the tasks that she had simply assumed: opening and sorting the mail, setting the agendas for council meetings, and so forth. But with Pastor Jane's coming, there was a new variable in the equation. Ruth realized how fragile were the traditions buttressing her power and how unstable was that power itself.

Weber's characteristics help to identify various facets of charismatic leadership. Most readers of the sociologist do not dispute them. They do, however, argue with Weber's negative assessment of the effects of charismatic leadership. Weber draws a virtual life portrait of Adolf Hitler. Accordingly, he warns against the hypnotic effect of charismatic leaders.

Weber might be challenged: Is all charismatic leadership doomed to domination? One can point to clear examples of the positive leadership Ruth had shown her congregation: initiating effective and dynamic adult Bible study programs that outlasted her departure, sustaining—at least for her tenure at St. Paul's—a congenial and engaged group of women. One can point to charismatic leaders whose leadership has had profound effect on the history of the twentieth century: Martin Luther King, Jr., Oscar Romero, Mahatma Gandhi, Mother Teresa.[11] The list would be endless. Is it the case that all charismatic power degenerates into domination? Or are there instances where the charisms of a gifted leader may have more beneficent issue?

Philosopher Dorothy Emmet challenges Weber's negative assessment of charismatic power directly. She counters:

> But is there not a real distinction between the kind of personal leader who exercises a kind of hypnotic power and is content to dominate people, and the kind of charismatist who is able to strengthen the will power of the people he influences, so that they make their own best effort in their own way? This may in the end lead to their thinking or working in a way quite different from his, and the charismatist will accept the fact that this may be so, though there may be stages when, like a trainer, he may subject them to disciplined guidance and direction. There may be stages in training when people must be subjected to "blind obedience." The real distinction is whether in the end they are allowed to graduate and are set free, or whether the leader keeps them subservient to himself.[12]

In effect, Emmet has distinguished two different kinds of charismatic leadership: the hypnotic charismatic leader and the inspirational charismatic leader. The distinction rests decisively on the effect of such leadership on the ones following: Is it directed toward domination or empowerment? Do the ones following feel overwhelmed or inspired? Are they mutely following the wishes of the leader or encouraged to think on their own?

Both the hypnotic charismatic leader and the inspirational charismatic leader are possessed of incredible "power within." The former uses that power to dominate; the latter, to educate, to energize, and to empower others. The effect of hypnotic leadership is slavery; the effect of inspirational leadership is freedom, freedom to work constructively on one's own. The people following a hypnotic leader are slaves; those following an inspirational leader are potential leaders themselves. In many ways, the inspirational charismatic leader is similar to a leader possessed of "power over" in the parental mode. The constraints on her power are the same constraints that are operative in this form of power: It must be temporary, not terminal; it must have as its end, creation of peers, not slaves.[13]

The situation at St. Paul's is an important example, not of simple hypnotic charismatic leadership, nor of simple inspirational charismatic leadership, but of how mixed is the effect of charismatic leadership on those under its sway. It would be easy to paint Ruth as the hypnotic charismatic leader. She is used to having devotees, both in the women's groups and in the congregation at large. Even the former pastor depended on her for "reading the pulse" of the congregation or discerning its corporate spirit. When she and Pastor Jane ran into public conflict, the other participants in the conversation were reduced to silence, unable to find their own way. Clearly, these are marks of a hypnotic charismatic leader.

Yet, there are other moments in the story that challenge this easy interpretation. Perhaps it was precisely Ruth's charismatic leadership that inspired the congregation to consider a woman pastor in the first place: a bold move for a group of people not easily given to progressive ideas! Perhaps it was Ruth's charismatic leadership that inspired a woman in her own circle to challenge her. Faced with Ruth's own summary conclusion that a group that could elect no president simply had to disband, the woman suggested that maybe they didn't even need a president for their denominational standing, provided they could decide who would represent them at which functions. This was clearly *not* the conclusion for which Ruth was pressing, but could it not have been the unseen issue of her own leadership? Ruth's charismatic leadership was far more ambiguous than it initially seemed. There may indeed be two kinds of charismatic leaders, with people fitting into one category or the other. But it may also be the case that any one person's charismatic leadership may have moments of both styles intermingled, as did Ruth's.

Keeping Charisma in Check

What then keeps the charismatic leadership more inspirational than hypnotic? Again, Dorothy Emmet turns to this question in her analysis of charismatic power and identifies three checks on charismatic power: self-knowledge, a sense of humor, and generosity.[14]

1. Self-knowledge is the ability to distinguish between the cause driving a movement and the self, an awareness of the effects of one's leadership on others, and a straightforward assessment of one's assets and liabilities. First, the ability to distinguish between the cause and the self is hard won and easily lost. Knowing the distinction and practicing it consistently require a tremendous amount of self-knowledge on the part of the charismatic leader—and his trusted confidantes. Without this first piece of self-knowledge, success of the movement is counted as personal gain; failure, as personal loss.

Ruth's self was so entangled in the whole inclusive language issue, that she would stake out *any* position on the issue that would secure her power and distinguish it from the power of her pastor. She was so enmeshed in her leadership of the women's circle, that she could not imagine how the group could continue without her physical presence. Both are negative examples of the importance of self-knowledge.

But a more positive instance of Ruth's self-knowledge concludes the story. Hearing Pastor Jane's farewell, which asked for the reconciliation of the Spirit of Christ between the two of them, it was Ruth, not her pastor, who initiated physically that reconciliation in an embrace.

Second, an effective charismatic leader needs to have a keen awareness of the effects of her leadership. In addition to self-knowledge, the charismatic leader needs to know the selves of the people whom she is leading. Are they slaves and devotees or potential peers? The hypnotic charismatic leader regards every potential peer as a future threat to his authority. The goal of this sort of leadership is unquestioning devotion, which masks unreflective obedience. The inspirational charismatic leader sees in an emerging leader the desired effect of her influence. These articulate vastly different perceptions of challenge and critique. The woman who spoke out against terminating the women's group would be perceived by a hypnotic charismatic leader as a complete threat, but by an inspirational charismatic leader as a welcome corrective.

Perhaps Pastor Jane, who was herself possessed of a great deal of charismatic power, is a good example here of inspirational charismatic leadership. Without judging, without using the word "racism," and without prescribing ways of addressing it, she pointed to two different ways of handling two different groups using the church's facilities. This allowed the council to name their own behavior and to begin to address it. Perhaps it was permission to name their own racism, rather than external judgment that produced a change of heart—and a change in behavior—on the part of council members toward the Origins students. Their marked shift in behavior triggered a conversion on the part of other congregational members. People went out of their way to be gracious to the Laotians.

Finally, the charismatic leader always needs to make a healthy and realistic assessment of her own assets and liabilities. Knowing what she can and cannot do creates habits which are critical to the charismatic leader, the habits of confidence and humility. An appropriate confidence sustains her in times of failure; a proper humility chastens her in times of success. Confidence is critical to inspirational leaders. It counters a perfectionism that often marks gifted people; it moves people out of the paralysis of perfection. So also humility is critical to inspirational leaders.[15] Perhaps we see humility best exemplified by Pastor Jane's truthful remarks to Ruth that they would probably never be able to "talk through" the differences between them and that it was beyond her own power to reconcile with Ruth, given such vast differences. Nonetheless, she claimed the reconciliation of the Spirit of Christ for the two of them—and was rightly confident in claiming that.

2. A sense of humor is an important asset for a charismatic leader, and this includes the ability to poke fun at oneself as well as the situation in which the group may find itself. Humor buttressed with self-knowledge enables one not to take oneself too seriously; humility always intervenes to expose the vulnerable edges. But humor also enables one not to take others too seriously; a healthy confidence intrudes as a kind of grounded lightheartedness in the tensest or darkest moments. Humor leavens a potential confrontation in the council member's dry query, "From the waist up or from the waist down?" The remark invited people to laugh at themselves and had the effect of alleviating the situation as a whole.

But humor has a political edge as well, evidenced daily in the work of political cartoonists, particularly in years with national conventions and a presidential campaign. Perhaps even more telling than the statistics from the latest poll would be a random sampling of editorial page images. It is not coincidence that the blind librarian in Umberto Eco's *The Name of the Rose* desperately guarded access to Aristotle's lost book on humor.[16] Humor destabilizes all authority, including that of a charismatic leader.

3. A final check on charismatic leadership is the spirit of generosity. A temptation in charismatic leadership is the desire to be the only one with the gifts. This creates a blindness to the gifts of others and to a diversity of gifts, all of which may be essential to sustaining the whole. A generous spirit allows others to emerge with distinctive and different approaches to a situation—even if the situation has already been resolved! Pastor Jane's use of inclusive language had in fact already been approved by congregational consensus. When Ruth raised the issue again, the pastor, rather than using a juridical appeal to the prior consensus, generously reopened discussion. The issue of this new discussion may have invited people to be more honest about their discomfort and certainly allowed for people, like Ruth, who had altered their positions, to speak. The solution to let each lector read whatever translation of the Bible was more comfortable to him was an important way of inviting different gifts in the congregation to emerge.

All charismatic leadership is exercised in and among a community, in this case, the congregation at St. Paul's. To be legitimate, to be effective, indeed, to be or exist at all, it requires the support and acknowledgment of a community. Perhaps this is the most powerful check on charismatic power: the community in which it is exercised. Without the backing of a community, the most magnetic leader falters. With the backing of a community, a charismatic leader can accomplish anything, and the historical specificity of "anything" can range from a Jonestown and an Auschwitz to a Woodstock or an Earth Summit. But to focus exclusively on the charismatic leader risks naming the responsibility of a community to follow, to resist, or to ignore entirely that leadership.

The community functions critically in this case study to confirm Ruth's leadership, to resist it, and finally to decide that it can manage without it. Ruth initiated vital projects in adult education which were affirmed by the congregation and which confirmed her leadership. When Pastor Jane began to resist her control of mail and agenda, the congregation tacitly supported that intervention. There was no one to whom Ruth could appeal for return of her power. Finally, as Ruth prepared to depart, she discovered that her women's group could manage without her. The paradox was that her leadership had been so effective, that she was no longer needed.

Charismatic Leadership in the Church

Consideration of the role of community in the exercise of charismatic power invites the entire discussion into the church. What are the problems and possibilities of charismatic leadership within the church?

We have seen many of them in the case under study. Ruth shows inspiration in her leadership, initiating vital programs and discussions that in fact survived her departure. But she also shows control in her leadership, a control that slips away with Jane's call to be pastor to the community. The effects of charismatic leadership appear to be mixed. It has all the problems and possibilities of other forms of leadership. On one hand, it can inspire and empower, creating a community that is open to change and welcoming of the stranger. On the other, it can dominate and control, creating a community that is anxious about change and lets in strangers only if they will use the back door to the church, the toilets in the rear, and the patio outside for their noon meals.

Images of God

As one looks at "power within," it is clear that a certain image of God forms and informs a ministry of "power within." God as Spirit is a familiar figure in ministry conducted within this mode. The image of God awakens us to the dynamic, creative, and destabilizing attributes of God and confronts us with a God who might still surprise us.

The power of this Spirit blows where it wills. It put words in the mouths of Jeremiah, visions before Isaiah, and dreams in the head of Nebuchadnezzar; it brooded over the waters of creation; it rained fire upon the crowd gathered at Pentecost; it descended like a dove upon Jesus at his baptism. We always see the Spirit in motion, and we always are arriving almost too late. The temptation of course is to capture, organize, and institutionalize the Spirit. Astounded to see Jesus talking to Moses and Elijah, Peter wanted to freeze the action and build shrines for the divine visitors. Paul names the gifts of the Spirit in 1 Corinthians 12:8-10: "To one is given through the Spirit the utterance of wisdom, and to another the utterance of knowledge according to the same Spirit, to another faith by the same Spirit, to another gifts of healing by the one Spirit, to another the working of miracles, to another prophecy, to another the discernment of spirits, to another various kinds of tongues, to another the interpretation of tongues." The gifts seem collected loosely around their source, the Spirit of God. A few verses later, however, Paul has organized these same gifts into a hierarchy of ministry: "And God has appointed in the church first apostles, second prophets, third teachers; then deeds of power, then gifts of healing, forms of assistance, forms of leadership, various kinds of tongues" (1 Cor. 12:28).

Can the Spirit be so enclosed? How can the institutions we create remain Spirit-filled? The answer to the first question is an emphatic *no!* The answer to the second, a cautious "with difficulty." The story of Balaam and his ass chastens all of us. A man respected for his spiritual gifts and shamanic powers is shown up by his ass! Did Balaam think he had a corner on spiritual power? Did he fail to look for the Spirit outside himself? and in the most ordinary places? from the most "irrelevant" parts of his quotidian world? These questions themselves destabilize all righteous confidence and erase any pious security. Clearly the only way to ascertain where the Spirit is blowing is constantly to test the wind, open our eyes, and listen to donkeys.

The challenge to ministry is clear. It is very dangerous to equate the working of the Spirit with the working of any institution and with the leadership of even the most charismatic of leaders. Yet, it is always a surprise to see the Spirit at work in the midst of our most common places, the communities of which we are a part, and the leadership even we might offer. The implicit exhortation is toward modesty and attention.

In an article written in the 1940s, H. Richard Niebuhr criticized what he saw as a Christocentrism in much American

Protestant theology and charged it with practicing a "monotheism of the Second Person of the Trinity."[17] In part what was missing was a thoroughgoing examination of the continuing work of the Spirit in Christian life. When it erupted into the mainline denominations in the sixties, the charismatic movement created quite an uproar. As in the early church, it revealed a "power within" that was not restricted to priests, clergy, or designated leaders. The one to whom the gift of tongues was momentarily and eloquently given may not have been a "duly called and ordained minister" of the particular church in which she was speaking! Spiritually enlightened laity began to flex a "power within." Like charismatic leadership, the charismatic movement itself was intense, but short-lived. Where it was routinized into weekly healing services and prayer meetings, it still persists. But it did serve to awaken churchfolk to the dynamic work of the Spirit in the life of the churches.

Images of Community

Every theory of power is implicitly a theory of community.[18] "Power over" delineates a particular sort of community. Sovereign images of God engender a community counseled toward obedience and cautioned against disobedience; parental images of God engender a community counseled toward honor and cautioned against dishonor and irreverence.[19] How would a community formed by the image of God as Spirit conduct itself?

Spirit images of God engender a community that is counseled to be open to and discerning of the gifts of God's Spirit and cautioned against rigidity and closemindedness. It would articulate a community that practiced, in the deepest sense, hospitality toward the stranger. The danger in a community operating in this mode would be instability and lack of boundaries.

These traits are all illustrated with both power and poignancy in the story of Ruth and Pastor Jane. Because Ruth is the "pulse of the congregation," her spirit becomes confused with the spirit of the congregation and the Spirit of God. She becomes the gatekeeper of congregational concerns; her judgment of what the congregation will and won't want to deal with is accepted without question. Her effect in these areas is that of a hypnotic charismatic leader. Pastor Jane tries to appeal to the spirit of the

95

congregation—and ultimately the Spirit of God—in an effort to engage in some sort of corporate discernment. Issues of boundaries surface whenever the Spirit of God is acknowledged, because the "Spirit blows where it wills." Boundary issues break into this congregation sharply as it tries to determine its linguistic borders in how it addresses God; as it tries to determine the spatial borders in how it allots space to a group that needs it, while maintaining the integrity of both groups; as it tries to practice hospitality to the stranger. The task of discerning God's Spirit and distinguishing it from the spirit of other charismatic leaders is a painful one, though not without humor, and it comes only through deliberate and prayerful self-reflection. It is poignant that, in this process of discerning the spirits, Ruth's charismatic power diminishes, and it is she who becomes the stranger. Pastor Jane finds that she is called to practice hospitality to the one who has attempted to estrange her from the congregation and alienate her leadership. For them both, she claims the reconciliation of nothing less than the Spirit of Christ.

Images of Leadership

A leader operating in this kind of "power within" mode would be acutely aware of her personal power or charisma within a group. A leader needs to engage in the practice of self-knowledge and assess realistically her peculiar configuration of assets and liabilities. Such an assessment, it is to be hoped, would make the charismatic leader cautious in regard to use and abuse of that power, but also bold in calling out and naming the dormant powers of the group and of the members within the group. The power of her charisma would serve initially to attract and then gradually move on to empower members of the group. This is charismatic leadership at its best.

Although it is clear that Ruth was reluctant to relinquish her stranglehold on the "pulse of the congregation," her leadership may have been more empowering to others than she herself had intended. Perhaps it was her singular leadership that moved the congregation to call a female pastor. Ironically, it is this other woman in a leadership capacity whom Ruth finds most threatening to her own authority. Perhaps it was her singular leadership that moved a woman to challenge her assumption that her departure would close down the women's group. Ironically, this is exactly the opposite reaction Ruth was seeking.

At the same time and as we have seen, charismatic leadership has its pitfalls and resulting caricatures. Too often the charismatic leader wants to be the only person in the group with the goods: the Fearless Leader. Rather than empower the group, the leader disempowers it, making it dependent on the "power within" the leader. While the leader exercises a power from within, the effect of such power—whether it is acknowledged by the group or not—is a classic form of "power over" in the warrior mode. Its unique form of oppression is impression: Dazzled by its charismatic leader, a group blindly and unquestioningly does whatever the leader wills, even to the point of following a command to commit suicide, as was the case in Jonestown. The caricature of the charismatic leader points to the real problems with a "power within" leadership, which then must be held in tension with its possibilities.

Power III

Power With
Coaction and Friendship

The Healers

Trinity Church is an urban congregation in a large southeastern city. There are 1300 active members and another 1200 members who are inactive but rostered. It is an affluent congregation which borders one of the oldest historical sectors of the city, a fashionable residential neighborhood, and a tough inner-city area which is the site of a low-income housing project.

The congregation has adjusted to its location well and initiated a number of ministries in the surrounding communities, which are sustained and directed by an active laity and a team of lay ministers. This ministry of the laity is supported by a clergy team of a priest and two associate rectors. Social ministries, task forces, and prayer chains extend the work of the church into the community.

Mary had long been a member of the congregation. It was her home congregation: there, she had participated in the lay ministry of the church; there, she had discerned a call to direct her theological education toward ordained ministry. After two years at seminary, she was asked by the congregation if she would consider a summer appointment. The priest would be on sabbatical; the two associate rectors would be staggering their vacations throughout the summer. Would she be willing to come on staff for the summer to provide some pastoral continuity? Mary accepted easily: She looked forward to being at her home congregation and with friends of long-standing.

Upon arrival, Mary met with the two associate rectors, and the three discussed her work for the summer. One of her chief responsibilities was the Thursday morning Healing Service and Eucharist. This had long been a part of the church's weekly roster of services, but attendance had fallen off and enthusiasm had waned. Mary's task was simple: to put "new energy" into the service. The rectors had no real specific suggestions as to how this might be done and no real concrete expectations as to what the service might accomplish. Mary was given a charge, a challenge, and the resources of the church for her work.

Mary had regularly attended the Healing Service and Eucharist as a member of the congregation about ten years before. Then and under the guidance of a young priest, the service had much energy and the participation of about fifty to sixty persons. Two lay ministers involved in the service had written a beautiful litany of healing, still used in the present service. Speaking in tongues would have been unusual for the group, even ten years before, but the priest, assisted by layfolk, had practiced laying on of hands and asked for prayers from the people for the people.

At the first service she attended upon her return, Mary noticed far fewer persons in attendance. A group of roughly fifty to sixty persons had dropped to about twenty to thirty. There was still lay participation: Two lay ministers walked in with the rector and sat opposite him in the chancel area, two steps removed from the congregation. One of the lay ministers read the litany for healing; the other read the prayer list, compiled of sick and ailing members of the congregation and community. The rector read the Bible and preached—all from the chancel area. The congregation was drawn largely from the church's senior constituency, predominantly female, with several of the congregants in wheelchairs. Several drivers were in attendance: women in their sixties who had helped to transport the elderly. There were a smattering of middle-aged women and an occasional person who had come as part of the church's outreach to the street people, the Direct Services Ministry.

The order of service was set:

> Opening Prayers
> Scripture
> Sermon
> Music
> Litany of Healing/Prayer List
> Anointing: once a month
> Offertory
> Eucharist
> Music
> Dismissal

The configuration of worship space was set.

Much of the liturgical activity took place in the chancel, which was raised two steps above the congregation. The rector preached from a lectern in the chancel. The rector celebrated at an altar which faced the wall and was two additional steps above the level of the chancel.

Mary was faced with a question. Given the order of service and the configuration of worship space, how could she put "new life" into the liturgy? She wanted the service to become a "liturgy," literally, a work of the people. As the service had grown, it had become "a work of the people" that seemed very distant from them. She wondered how close it was to their needs.

With these questions in the back of her mind, Mary led her first Thursday service. When it came time for the sermon, Mary walked past the lectern and down the stairs from the chancel into the nave. What was not in her memory, she had committed to notecards, so that she was not bound by the need to have a lectern in front of her. This modest alteration in worship space certainly created some "life"! When people accustomed to a certain distance between themselves and their worship leader saw Mary trespass it, they perked up instantly. But her gentle manner and consoling presence provided the needed measure of assurance. Gradually, people were able to fall into the message of the sermon.

At the offertory Mary paused again. Again, she moved from the chancel into the nave. This time she had not notecards but an offering plate full of small, folded slips of blue paper. She began to speak: "This morning, instead of putting something *into* the offering plate, I invite you to take something out of it. On each slip of paper, I've put the name of one of the people on our prayer list. I'd like to pass this around, and you may take one slip or several or no slip at all: whatever the Spirit moves you to do. During the days that follow, hold this person up in your prayers. Put the name on your refrigerator or in your Bible or on your night table—wherever you will see it frequently. As you move through your week, as you do your weekly devotions, I would simply ask that you hold this person up in your prayers. If any names are left over, I will put them on my desk." When she finished speaking, she took out a blue slip of paper for herself and then passed the offering plate to an older woman in the front pew, who accepted it in quiet amazement. The plate went around the nave in utter silence, coming to rest on a credence back by the baptismal font, where people could walk by it on their way out of the chapel. When Mary retrieved the plate after the service, there were no blue slips of paper in it.

The next Healing Service and Eucharist was exactly a week away; yet as soon as the congregants got home, the church telephone began ringing. "My blue slip of paper says 'Charles.' Can you tell me what Charles' specific prayer needs are?" Mary and the church secretary tried their best to answer the various requests and track down information as it was needed, as it was available, and as it was appropriate to share with the intercessor. They found that some of the people who had long been on the prayer list had died, moved away, or been placed in rest homes nearer their children. They found that others had passed this health crisis in their lives and were no longer in need of the intercessions of the community. Mary's gesture certainly proved to be a way to update the prayer list! But more than that, it connected people with one another. They found themselves thinking about the name on their blue slips of paper—and wanting to know more than the name. Another question frequently asked was, "Well, how old is Ella Mae?" Ignorant of the answer and somewhat exasperated by the question, the secretary taking the call countered, "My goodness! what does it matter!" "Oh, it matters a lot!" said the voice at the other end, seemingly indignant with such insensitivity. "I would pray differently for a child undergoing surgery than I would for an eighty-year-old undergoing surgery."

Phone calls poured into the church throughout the week. After the initial queries for information about the names they'd received, people began suggesting the names of others who needed intercession: "Alma Jean is having surgery on Monday. Can she be put on the prayer list?" "Mary Elizabeth is grieving and needs our prayers." The names all went on blue slips of paper and into the offering plate on Mary's desk.

At the service the following week the offering plate was full of blue slips, and the energy that met their dispersal indicated new investment in a part of the service that had traditionally been a mere recitation of names. As her sermon text, Mary chose verses from the epistle of James: "Are any among you suffering? They should pray. Are any cheerful? They should sing songs of praise. Are any among you sick? They should call for the elders of the church and have them pray over them, anointing them with oil in the name of the Lord"

(James 5:13-14). After the sermon and before the litany of healing, Mary remained in the nave. "You also came here this morning out of your need, and we all have needs. Many of you know that my parents are both quite ill. You have expressed your concern to me about them, and I need your support. Janet [a lay minister who usually assisted with the service], who was not able to be with us today, said that I could share with you the reason why. Her mother is also very sick. I want to know what *your* prayer needs are."

From the back of the church a woman spoke up: "I'm having surgery next Tuesday at St. Joseph's Medical Center, and I'm scared. I need your prayers for me on Tuesday." Almost before she had finished, another spoke up: "I'm having a procedure at the same hospital on Tuesday also. I'll be there praying for you, and the rest of you can pray for both of us." A ripple of laughter had to subside before the next woman spoke: "My friend Rufus Johnson has a brain tumor, and he needs your prayers, too." Mary paused to write these new names down, then she looked up: "We will all be praying for all of you."

After the first month of Mary's leadership, she called together the two lay ministers, Janet and another woman, for some assessment and evaluation. The three of them talked about the structure and shape of the worship service, the extra burden its success was placing on the church secretaries, who were constantly fielding calls for the service, and agreed these indicated a need for a more organized prayer ministry in the church.

The three scheduled a meeting with one of the associate rectors in charge of pastoral ministry. He received their proposal with a single question, and it was directed to Mary: "How will this continue after you're gone?" It was an unexpected question, but it was still not one whose answer Mary could in confidence predict. The women proposed to gather a group of people with a long-term and already identified interest in the needs of the elderly and see if they would take immediate responsibility for the service and the concerns it surfaced. With the rector's knowledge and with his suggestions for interested parties, they proceeded.

Identifying these people involved a lot of telephone work during a season in which people were themselves on vacation or traveling. As she worked, Mary began to suspect that this could be the foundation for a larger prayer ministry that would provide a spiritual basis for the many programs in which members were involved. She knew also that the first concrete piece would be to work with an already established desire to expand ministry with and to the elderly.

When she gathered a significant number of committed people, Mary called a "generative meeting." She began the meeting with a confession: "I called this meeting, and I don't know what to do. However, we're here because we're concerned about an important aspect of this church's ministry: its ministry to the elderly." Mary had to make further disclaimers: "I can't do this, because I'm going to be leaving in six weeks. And I can't even tell you how to do it, because you need to discover what will work for you and what you're willing to support." As the meeting progressed, two co-chairs were elected: one a seventy-year-old woman and the other a thirty-five-year-old woman. Their chief task was to find interested and committed prayer ministers to cover the various age groups in the congregation.

The discussion focused on the Healing Service and Eucharist itself: Was this working? How might it work better? Initially, the group didn't feel that it had the authority to make any changes in the liturgy: "The liturgy is The Liturgy," said one man. "Who are we to change it?" There was widespread agreement with his statement, until an eighty-three-year-old woman and long-time member of the parish piped up, "Wait a minute! Remember Father Branston? When he used to pray, he came down and knelt in the aisle facing the altar." She got people thinking. Finally, Janet burst out: "You know, the problem with the service is that everything happens *up there*. Those are *our* people and *our* prayers. They ought to be down here with *us!*"

The room was suddenly quiet. Janet's eyes were bright. Mary paused, then asked, "What would that look like? How would that happen?" After animated discussion, the group decided that the lay ministers should sit in the congregation, not up in the chancel, and should sit in pews on either side of the congregation, so that they could face the people when reading the prayer lists. The decision was implemented in the next and all subsequent services.

Before the meeting concluded, Mary asked: "Now, what you're taking on is a heavy responsibility. How will *you* be fed? How will *you* grow in prayer? Who will minister to the ministers?" The group drew a corporate blank, looking again to Mary to do this or at least to tell them how to do it. She laughed and said simply:

"We don't have to have all the answers at this meeting—I did say it was a 'generative meeting,' not a 'definitive' one. I could imagine you going off on retreats together, having prayer groups among yourselves, whatever. But you'll need to be attentive to your own needs, and see what will best meet them."

The energy expressed in the 'generative' meeting was transplanted into the service. A carpool network ferried people to and from the services. Many of the parishioners visited each other in home and hospital, as they moved through illness and recovery together. People exchanged phone numbers for conversation during the rest of the week. The liturgy was becoming the work of the people.

As the summer drew to a close, both associate rectors were invited to preach in the Thursday morning liturgy. They were variously comfortable with the new space of worship. One returned to the lectern for his sermon, while the other brought a music stand down into the nave for his sermon notes. Both noticed and commented on the energy of the service and pledged full support. Mary departed for the beginning of fall semester with a feeling of accomplishment coupled with regret at leaving behind her friends and her ministry.

When she returned the following summer, she arrived Wednesday and attended unannounced the Thursday morning Healing Service and Eucharist. The service looked much as it had when she'd first attended it the previous summer. The lay ministers were up in the chancel sitting across from the priest; the sermon was preached from the pulpit; there were no blue slips. The only remnant of the enthusiasm of the past summer was a few moments before the service, when the priest asked the congregation for names of those who'd been ill or in need of prayer. These he wrote on a list and incorporated into the prayer list, which was, as it had always been, read by one of the lay ministers.

"Power Within" and "Power With"

The story of the Healers reveals a leadership situation with many facets. The dynamic of space dominates any analysis of the situation. A worship space that had been apart from the people is literally re-presented as a space that is with them, among them, and indeed, theirs. This shift in spatial dynamics signals a shift in naming as well. Congregants for whom healing is sought become themselves the healers. The ones for whom prayers are offered become themselves the pray-ers. The sick become shamans for one another. Michael Taussig speaks of the relationship between the shaman and the healer as one that creates power: ". . . between the figure who sees but will not talk of what he sees, and the one who talks, often beautifully, but cannot see. It is this that has to be worked through if one is to become a healer."[1] What is the power that exists in the interstices between shaman and healer?

This final form of power is "power with," or, in the words of Mary Parker Follett, "coactive power."[2] "Power with" is sometimes known as the power of solidarity or strength in numbers, and it is usually manifest in people who have far greater power together than any one of them has individually. It is the power of a grass roots movement, the power of a labor union, the power of any group that dares to articulate a common purpose and a common good.

The story of the Healers presents several compelling illustrations of "power with." It is the power that poured into the church office, as people who'd attended the Thursday morning Healing Service and Eucharist began calling to identify the people attached to the names on their blue slips of paper and their specific prayer needs. It is the power of a group gathered to address the ministry to the elderly and discovering that they can bring their lay ministers down into the pews with them. It is the power of an old woman, with myriad health problems of her own, taking up the responsibility to pray for a sick neighbor.

This particular form of power need not be galvanized by charismatic leaders, but the best charismatic leaders create "power with" in the groups following them, as they call out and name the power which all share in common. Inspirational charismatic leadership, tempered by humor, humility, and self-knowledge, creates a "power with" in the groups in which it appears. Indeed, it is at this point that "power within" and "power with" coalesce. A lay minister articulated this moment of empowerment: "Those are *our* people and *our* prayers. They ought to be down here with us!" Mary's inspirational leadership had both enabled and empowered this conclusion. That spirit of solidarity carried the prayer meetings through the summer.

But what happened after Mary's departure? Was the group too dependent on her leadership? Had she infused an "energy" into the service that was hers alone and would disappear after she left? Was there, in fact, something going on in the service when she started her summer at Trinity, which, in their quest for "new energy," she and the rectors might have missed, and which quietly reasserted itself after her departure? Coactive power could possibly have been at work in the service as Mary had found it, albeit in a much less intimate and engaged fashion. The questions point to a complex relationship between charismatic and coactive power and raise only another question: Who identifies the power of friendship?

Possibilities of "Power With"

Examples of coactive power appear throughout history. This is probably the kind of power Jesus intended to impute to his rowdy crowd of disciples, though each of them kept vying with the others for a special seat of honor beside their Lord. The mother of the "sons of thunder," James and John, seems restive with such egalitarianism, and seeks special honor for her progeny. This is only one of a number of apostolic debates on greatness.[3] Jesus responds with a baffling series of reversals, which value children the same as adults, neighbor the same as self, and finally place the last above the first. The establishment of expected hierarchies did not correspond to this kind of "power with."

And, lest leaders always be charged with the establishment of hierarchy, the story of the Healers offers its own reversal. In the "generative meeting," we see how difficult shared power is to choreograph. The people are more than ready to let their leader, Mary, be in charge, and they look to her repeatedly for the word that she will take care of things for them—or, failing that, that she will at least tell them how to take care of things for themselves. With no small amount of persistence, Mary continually throws the questions and the leadership back to the group: "What do you want? What do you need? What will you support? How will you be fed?"

"Power with" is often presented in monastic communities, which strived to live under a rule and under the guidance of an abbot. The Rule of St. Benedict presented itself as "a little Rule for beginners,"[4] but those "beginners" were people who lived in community and shared a common life of work, prayer, and praise.

Benedict identified four kinds of monks, two of which were solitary spiritual virtuosi (sarabaites and gyratory monks). A third kind, anchorites, had prepared themselves "in the fraternal line of battle for the single combat of the hermit." The fourth kind of monk, the cenobites, gathered in community under a rule and an abbot, practiced a life of spiritual friendship, and were, in the eyes of Benedict, "the best kind of monk."[5]

Many see the modern feminist movement as an exercise in "power with." Strong charismatic leadership initiated the women's movement, but that leadership has largely been directed to motivating and empowering a larger group. Not surprisingly, feminist scholars have done ground-breaking work on the subject of "power with" or friendship, and feminist philosopher Janice Raymond articulates clearly why:

> Over the past two decades, we have seen that, indeed sisterhood is powerful. There have emerged rape crisis centers, battered women's shelters, feminist bookstores, women's health clinics, feminist journals and magazines, Women's Studies programs, and all sorts of women's conferences. All of these programs and all of these ventures generated a sisterly solidarity, but many of them also failed because, in my opinion, there was nothing to hold them together beyond what I call the communion of resistance. Unfortunately, sisterhood that was created in the struggle against all forms of male tyranny did not mean that women became friends, that they shared a common world beyond the struggle.[6]

For Raymond and others, sisterhood practiced a "power against" and formed "communions of resistance," but friendship practices a "power with" and moves toward the vision and implementation of a common good.

The civil rights movement is another case in point. Martin Luther King, Jr., was a strong charismatic leader. Yet the movement did not die with him. He gave language to the hopes and visions of a huge sector of people, black and brown and white, rich and poor, male and female. His dream of equality became theirs, and the power of a charismatic leader inspired others to continue working to realize the dream in various arenas.

Finally, Twelve-Step programs provide a fascinating study in the translation of "power over" into "power with." The ticket of admission into any one of a variety of groups is acknowledgment of one's own powerlessness. The demons that drive someone may be legion: alcohol, cocaine, other drugs, gambling, relationships, sex, and so on, but the ticket to recovery is always the same. Confessing one's own powerlessness is a foundational confession, and making it in the context of a group of people who are similarly disempowered creates a solidarity in the struggle, a sense of corporate strength, and a power in the group connected to a Higher Power.

"Power with" is a very real and important force within our lives. Certainly, the congregation at the Healing Service and Eucharist moved from the powerlessness of illnesses into a shared power of healing. A community of the sick people *to whom* ministry is directed became itself a community of ministry. The lepers became healers. The story stands as a powerful witness to the powers embodied in a corporate good and a common vision.

Problems of "Power With"

And yet, lest we embrace too enthusiastically this form of power, there are pitfalls here as well. In his delightful book *Four Loves*, C. S. Lewis identifies the exclusionary tendencies of friendship or coactive power. He detects a "pride" in friendship, "whether Olympian, Titanic, or merely vulgar," and he proceeds to explain why: "Friendship must exclude. From the innocent and necessary act of excluding to the spirit of exclusiveness is an easy step; and thence to the degrading pleasure of exclusiveness."[7] There is a seductive elitism in the close bonding of people—especially to those left on the outside. Friendship, or "power with," has clear exclusionary tendencies.

In her book *Money, Sex, and Power*, feminist philosopher Nancy Hartsock identifies another danger of shared power: political amorphism. Looking retrospectively at the feminist movement, she observes an understandable but dangerous allergy among women to the two kinds of power which have oppressed them the most: dominative power, or "power over" in its warrior mode, and hypnotic charismatic leadership, or "power within" in its dominative mode. In an effort to avoid any use of power that has historically abused women, feminists fell into another trap: a kind of personal, structureless politics; widespread opposition to leadership of any kind; an insistence on working collectively; and an emphasis on process, often to the exclusion of getting things done.[8]

Certainly, the story of the Healers is a powerful and positive illustration of "power with" or coactive power, and it is difficult to see immediate evidence of these darker aspects of coactive power: either its exclusionary tendencies or the danger of political amorphism. Yet, alongside the positive transformative power of space, liturgy, and prayer, there are hints of both these aspects. Perhaps the exclusionary tendencies of coactive power are suggested (but only suggested!) in the guise of an ownership that could tend toward possession. Janet's insight in the "generative meeting" is beautiful—and gives one pause. "Those are *our* people and *our* prayers." Suddenly, prayers can be possessed, can be possessions; suddenly, space is delineated as "theirs," belonging to the ordained ministers, and "ours," belonging to the laity. Coactive power, for all its positive attributes, often functions in opposition to another group that has traditionally held power or has been around longer or has simply exercised power overtly. An easy reaction to a familiar exclusion is to adopt it. The laywoman's words allude to this exclusionary tendency.

Political amorphism can only be read in the part of the story that is not told. Between Mary's summer appointment and the following summer, the Healing Service and Eucharist reverted to its original state. Was it again in need of "new energy"? or had the leaders missed seeing a quiet energy that had been there all along? What happened to the energized and committed group of laypeople who were going to shape a prayer ministry for the entire church? Did the "new energy" for the project depart with Mary? Did the proposal receive adequate support from the pastoral team? What had kept these people from doing something they had said they wanted done? Mary and the others had tried to design a structure so that the project would not rely on personalities. At its "generative meeting" the group had tried to articulate goals and procedures for meeting them, so that they could realize their vision. But, despite these steps, nothing remained the following summer. So it seems that "power with" or friendship is an ambivalent form of power, with problems and possibilities for community.

Aspects of "Power With" or Friendship

What is "power with" or coactive power? Perhaps coactive power is best understood by examining another phenomenon with which it is often equated: friendship. Friendship seems to be both ubiquitous and undefinable. Certainly all of us *have* friends and *are* friends in some vague way. That's the ubiquitous part. But what about the undefinable? When pressed further to elaborate on the subject of friendship, our minds turn as blank as the greeting cards in that section of card shops labeled "friendship."

To find out about friendship or coactive power, move back in time, to other centuries wherein people had more to say about friendship: fourth-century Athens or the Roman Republic or a lonely monastery in the Yorkshire moors during the twelfth century.[9] To find out about the power that is friendship, we need to imagine that we could look at greeting cards from these other centuries and see what these other people have had to say about it. If this imaginary historical survey could be completed, it would, I suspect, suggest that there are several facets of coactive power or friendship: choice, similarity, mutuality, equality, reciprocity, benevolence, and knowledge.

First, the power of friendship is a matter of choice. Simply put, we choose our friends; we choose these people with whom we will be in relationship. That seems a statement of the obvious, until we consider how many intimate relationships in which we are enmeshed, over which we have little or no choice. Certainly, we have no choice over who it is that our parents are; nor do we choose brothers or sisters. We can't choose who our children will be or become. We don't choose parents or siblings or children the way one chooses laundry detergent. Indeed, these people are often like utter strangers to us, people whom we could not say we either know or perhaps even want to know. We can choose to befriend our parents, our children, our siblings, but friendship is not necessarily a part of that relationship.

We have more choice over our romantic partners, our husbands and wives, our mates and partners, but even here there is an involuntary element in these alliances that could be described only as chemistry or "spark." Too many people we know, like ourselves perhaps, have remarkably bad choice in these sorts of relationships. All rational argument will move in favor of breaking out of a relationship that is patently a bad choice, but something makes one stay, almost unwillingly. We can choose to befriend our partners, but it is not necessarily part of the relationship.

Friendship is quite different from these other relationships, in that friendship is a voluntary relationship. We *choose* our friends. Indeed, it is this terrible element of choice that so frightened parents in those delicate years of adolescence. As the parents retained less and less choice over who were to be their daughter's friends, as she gained more and more choice, they feared that she would not choose well. Choice is an element of friendship. Janice Raymond alludes to the importance of choice by noting its absence in the early stages of the women's movement. Being sisters in the cause did not necessarily confer friendship; indeed, it often put one with women who were strangers. "Unfortunately, sisterhood that was created in the struggle against all forms of male tyranny did not mean that women became friends, that they shared a common world beyond the struggle. Sisterhood did not automatically create a private and public space where female friendship could occur."[10] Creating a "communion of resistance" did not necessarily create a circle of friends.

Choice is one of those difficult aspects of congregational life. One can choose to join a specific denomination or church, but for others denominational identity is not at all a matter of choice. This was expressed well by a lesbian seeking ordination in a church that refused it to practicing homosexuals. After being told by a synodical official to seek ordination in a church that did not refuse ordination to practicing homosexuals, she exploded: "As if my Lutheranism were any more a matter of choice than my sexual orientation!" Denominational affiliation may or may not be a matter of choice, and literature on congregational life ranges from dubbing the congregation "a company of strangers" to "a community of friends."[11]

Certainly, we do not choose the person sitting next to us in the pew. Yet, in this story of the Healers, choice is present. Outside the ordinary schedule of worship, the Thursday worship service was one that people could choose to attend. Mary chose to meet with the two lay ministers to engage in an initial evaluation of the service, and the three identified a group of people who chose to participate in a "generative meeting" which would explore further possibilities of a prayer ministry with the elderly. That group chose their own leaders: two co-chairs. Choice, then, was operative in the founding of a coactive network at Trinity church.

A second element of "power with" or friendship is similarity.

Friends have something in common: the same neighborhood, the same upbringing, the same block, the same sports, the same sense of humor, the same appreciation for good food or good wine or good jokes—or even bad food or bad wine or bad jokes. Friends have similar tastes—or lack thereof. And lack of taste can be an important glue in friendship. Friends are folk with whom one can get "down and dirty," with whom one can share a raunchy joke, a raunchy movie, a raunchy mood. Friends have something in common.

The similarities among those in the prayer ministry at Trinity are striking. Most of them were themselves ill or disabled and drawn to a healing service out of their own needs. The majority of them were elderly, and a large proportion of them were women. None of these groups—the ill and disabled, the elderly, or the women—was a group that had enjoyed easy access to the ecclesiastical structures of power. Perhaps it was not at all surprising that their similarities would draw a group like this to explore the power of friendship. Each had more power as part of a whole, than any did individually.

A third element is related to similarity, but distinct in important ways: mutuality. Similarity suggests that friends *have* in common certain things; mutuality suggests that friends *hold* in common certain things. While similarity suggests that friendships form around common interests or common characteristics, mutuality suggests that friendships form around common commitments. While similarity means that we two like to do this together, mutuality means that we two believe in this together. Mutuality suggests that friendships form around a common good.

For Aristotle, friendship was the civic glue. "Friendship also seems to hold states together,"[12] he muses, almost baffled by the reality of what he saw around him. He had identified the importance of mutuality. Perhaps Aristotle would be even more baffled if he were to experience political life in the United States today. In *Habits of the Heart*, Robert Bellah and his colleagues lament the lack of mutuality in our common life and suggest that this is part of our national heritage: a nation of individuals that has a hard time defining and committing itself to a common good that is something more than individual wholeness and therapeutic health. Noting that Aristotle categorized friendships as being based on pleasure, utility, and common commitments, the authors comment, "It is easy for us to understand the components of pleasure and usefulness, but we have difficulty seeing the point of considering friendship in terms of common moral commitments."[13] Perhaps this is part of the reason that we have trouble giving friendship any more definition than does the prose in greeting cards: "A friend is someone who likes you." More than liking, more than merely *having* something in common, friends *hold* something in common. Mutuality was a strong driving force behind the Healers' prayer ministry. The group that assembled for the "generative meeting" created the vision of a foundational spirituality that could inform and undergird the various social ministries in which the church was already engaged. The common vision galvanized the group and motivated it to begin thinking of changes in something they had never thought of changing: making the liturgy once again "the work of the people."

A fourth aspect of "power with" is equality. Friends are people who are equal in power, in status, in professional rank, in age. Friends are people who are peers. From a twentieth century perspective, it's curious to see Aristotle puzzle over whether or not husband and wife can be friends, because it reminds one of the inferior status of women throughout the classical world.[14] But his puzzlement also reminds us of the importance of equality in friendship. Aristotle is actually wrestling with the aspect of equality.

It is a struggle all too common to leaders. May a leader befriend this one? What about all the others? Does not the peerage of friendship countermand the very real imbalances of power that permeate the relationship between follower-leader, parishioner-pastor, student-teacher, employee-employer? In this arena, may I assume friendship, when in another situation I must be teacher? or pastor? or employer? May I engage in a relationship that demands peerage in this arena, when in another situation we must engage in a relationship that is, for better and for worse, hierarchical?

Friendships in the workplace or in the congregation or in the academy must always face the problem of equality, for friendship demands a relationship among equals, if it is not to slip into patronage or parentilization. Whether presumed or conferred in the relationship itself, friends are equals.

Equality figures in the story of the Healers in an interesting fashion. Certainly part of the generative group's eagerness to defer all questions to Mary was their accurate sense of her superior expertise. After all, she had the seminary training, the administrative abilities, the pastoral sensibilities. Her resistance to the group's desire that she take charge was in part a commitment to a project that was conceived, governed, and administered by equals.

A fifth aspect of friendship is related to equality: reciprocity. Friendship demands an equal giving and receiving among the parties involved. One person isn't always making sacrifices and the other always demanding them. One person isn't always giving—and unable to receive. One person isn't always receiving or, better, taking—and unable to give. There is equal giving and receiving on all sides in friendships.

Utility has been under fire as an aspect of friendship, yet reciprocity does make a place for utility in friendship. You need this one, and this one needs you, if only for something so simple as someone with whom to get "down and dirty." In itself, utility is a facet of friendship, so long as the needs are equal.

Problems arise when one person is more needy than the other. In many conversations with friends and acquaintances, one of the most consistent problems about relationships revolves around reciprocity: "I felt like I was being used . . . " or "I just wasn't getting enough out of the relationship." These are common enough litanies, and they all stem from the issue of reciprocity.

Reciprocity is a neuralgic issue in Christian communities, so committed are they to altruistic giving. It is Mary who introduces and reintroduces the matter of reciprocity. In a service that has turned those in need of healing into healers, Mary reminds the healers that they too need comfort. Again, in the "generative meeting" Mary tries to keep this question of reciprocity before the group. As the group begins to envision a church-wide prayer ministry, which it would initiate and support, Mary raises the question of reciprocity: "How will *you* be fed? How will *you* grow in prayer?" She knows the caregivers often need care themselves.

A sixth aspect of the power that is friendship is that of benevolence. Benevolence involves loving the other for herself alone. This aspect cuts against any utilitarian tendencies in reciprocity. Recognizing that friends do need each other, benevolence is the ability to say finally: "I love you, not because I need you, nor because you need me, but because you are you." Benevolence says exactly that, and benevolence pushes us beyond that actively to wish well for the other. Indeed, "benevolence" means literally "to wish well." Thomas Aquinas is adamant that true friendship demands this quality.

It is not every love that has the character of friendship but only the love which includes benevolence, by which we love someone so as to will some good for him. When we do not will good for the things we love, but seek their good for ourselves, as we do when we love wine, or a horse, or something of the kind, this is not the love of friendship, but a kind of concupiscence. It would indeed be ridiculous to say that one had friendship with wine, or with a horse.[15]

Friendship or coactive power involves benevolence. Certainly, benevolence figures importantly in the story of the Healers. Once the parishioners were allowed to be actively involved in the service of healing, once they were active agents of healing and not mere passive recipients of healing, they became involved in one another's lives. The phone calls to the church expressed concern about the well-being of another. Suddenly, this concern mattered greatly, concern best expressed in the words of an indignant, but benevolent woman calling into the church secretary: "I would pray differently for a child undergoing surgery than I would for an eighty-year-old undergoing surgery."

A final aspect of friendship is that of knowledge. We know our friends and by our friends are known. Friendship involves and invites subjectivity; friendship is a commitment both to prove and to be proved, to receive the self of the other and to become a self in the presence of another. This aspect of friendship reminds us that a true friendship involves truth: telling the truth about oneself and telling the truth of the other, when the other cannot see it.

How distant this aspect of truth is from our notions of friendship! If we were to ask someone in this last gasp of the twentieth century the opposite of friend, she would reply without hesitation, "enemy." If we were to ask someone in the classical world the same question, the reply, again without hesitation, would be, "flatterer." The opposition would have been clear: A friend tells you the truth; a flatterer tells you lies.

Reflecting on the truth-speaker, or parrhesiast, Michel Foucault notes that the role involves risk and danger: "Parrhesia is linked to courage in the face of danger: it demands the courage to speak the truth in spite of some danger."[16] The danger in the case under study was the risk of vulnerability. As the prayer ministry progressed, people were more and more open with their own needs and their own physical, emotional, and spiritual illnesses. Mary consciously initiated this herself in the second service, alluding publicly to her parents' illness and alluding, with her permission, to Janet's mother. In doing so, she allowed herself to be known by the group and to be present in their prayers. The people responded in kind, sharing their various fears and troubles, asking for compassion and understanding, making themselves known to one another.

Choice, similarity, mutuality, equality, reciprocity, benevolence, and knowledge: These are the salient characteristics of friendship. They inform this third kind of power, "power with" or coactive power.

A Ministry of Friendship

Ministry conducted in this mode has unique problems and possibilities. "Power with" does resonate—and resonate strongly—with certain facets of charity, or the love that is intended to mark Christians. Certainly mutuality or the pursuit of a common good is central to both friendship and charity. Mutuality is defined for the community in baptism and nurtured through word and sacrament. Benevolence, too, is a key fact of our calling as Christians and our ministries in the world. Charity practices benevolence in nothing less than acting in love and service to the neighbor.

But there are other elements of friendship or "power with," which would seem to be in direct and desperate conflict with Christian charity: choice, similarity, equality, reciprocity, and knowledge, and these conflicts are critical.

What about choice? We choose our friends; by our friends, we are chosen. But what about the man lying beaten by the side of the road in the Samaritan's path? What about the woman panhandling outside the Bank of America yesterday? What about the people in your congregation? What about the people who gathered on Thursday mornings for the Healing Service and Eucharist at Trinity? These people didn't choose to be together. In fact, if they had any choice, they would probably choose to be well and in need of no healing whatsoever.

Friendship would not seem to obligate people, who did not choose to be together in the first place, to one another. But charity offers different counsel. Charity demands that we aid one another regardless of the choice or who made it. Charity demands equal attention to all.

It was this aspect of choice that proved so destructive to religious life and communities of faith. "Particular friendships" were discouraged precisely because they fractured the community along lines of who was chosen and who was not. Choice gave way to an exclusionary spirit that was seen to be antithetical to a spirit of charity, which was supposed to hold sway in communities of faith.

What about similarity? What do church people have in common? In previous decades, we held much in common: a common history, common confirmation classes or First Communion dates, a shared history of baptisms and marriages and funerals, a common community and the space on which it was constructed. Yet, in many parts of this country, communities have dispersed. Old people have moved out; new people have replaced them. The sense of continuity and the store of common experiences have diminished. Many people in church on a given Sunday may not have grown up in that denomination, but been shaped by another tradition—or no religious tradition at all. Perhaps this is why many inner-city congregations are marked by such a high liturgical style: having failed to find among the membership many similarities in religious upbringing, these churches have moved increasingly toward a worship experience that is equally foreign to all. Similarity among a worshiping constituency is harder and harder to find, more and more difficult to assume.

What about equality? Here again is another point of friction. Friendship demands equality, so much so that the friend has often been described as another self. The pastor-parishioner relationship may boast of equality through baptism into the priesthood of all believers, but in the congregation there are differences between pastor and parishioner or between leader and follower in terms of role and function. To ignore these differences would be an act of denial. Today a pastor and a parishioner may share a morning of coffee and laughter together, but tomorrow the pastor will commune or marry her, baptize her child or bury her father. Situations in which the peerage of friendship is appropriate and situations in which the difference in role and function is appropriate need to be clearly defined and mutually acknowledged.

What about reciprocity? Friendship demands some equal giving and receiving, and without this there is whining. Charity would silence these complaints. Charity always counsels going the extra mile, turning the second cheek, giving not simply the cloak, but the shoes off one's feet and the shirt off one's back.

What of knowledge? Friends demand to know the other and to be by the other known. Friends tell each other the truth. Accordingly, one of the sins in friendship is betrayal, denying that you know the other, denying who the other is. Jesus gives anguished voice to the broken bond of their friendship in the Garden of Gethsemane: "Friend, do what you are here to do" (Matt. 26:50). Peter only repeats the sin in friendship, intensifying his denial with each query: "I do not know the man" (Matt. 26:72). Charity operates without knowledge and without this measure of truth; this is why so many "charitable contributions" are anonymous. Friendship demands revelation of a self.

Preference, similarity, equality, reciprocity, and knowledge: With these aspects of friendship charity is absolutely in conflict. Charity is nonpreferential, always giving, without demanding to receive or to know what the other is up to. Think of the conflict in a congregational setting: choosing to befriend a family or a person out of all the rest of the families in the church, sharing all the delights and frustrations of congregational life with someone, engaging in the simple givings and receivings of friendship with that family or that person, knowing this person or that family in ways that you can't and indeed don't even want to know the others. All this is a formula for faction within a congregation and for friction among its members. Such are the problems with this form of power in ministry.

Images of God

Yet we gain some insight into the possibility and the necessity of coactive power by examining one of its biblical models: the friendship of Jesus. A certain image of God forms and informs a ministry of "power with": the image of God as Friend. There is witness to this in the Gospel of John:

> This is my commandment, that you love one another as I have loved you. No one has greater love than this, to lay down one's life

for one's friends. You are my friends if you do what I command you. I do not call you servants any longer, because the servant does not know what the master is doing; but I have called you friends, because I have made known to you everything that I have heard from my Father. (John 15:12-15)

Here an old relationship is superseded by a new one. Servanthood, the master-slave relationship, is rejected as the one characterizing divine-human relationships. Rather, friendship is offered—and offered by God!—as the new relationship with God that Jesus reveals. The difference appears to be precisely the facets of mutuality and benevolence that knowledge of God through Jesus confers. A servant obeys blindly; he has no idea what is the intent of the one commanding. In friendship, however, obedience is locked into mutuality and knowledge, that is, commitment to a common vision of the kingdom of God and knowledge of the God whom Jesus Christ reveals.

Suddenly, other words about Jesus make a different kind of sense. Why was he rejected? Why was he the object of derision by Pharisees and Sadducees? There were many reasons, but one of the biggest was his friendship, his active practice of coactive power with the wrong people. "Behold," they had jeered, "a glutton and a drunkard, a friend of tax-collectors and sinners!" We remember that in the biblical world, you ate and drank with friends, and your friends were the people with whom you ate and drank. Suddenly, the worn-out sneer has new meaning: Jesus ate with the marginalized of his society; he drank with them; therefore, he was their friend. The jeer works as some revelatory equation. Jesus was crucified for the power he shared with others.

The friendship that Jesus modeled tells us some very important things about our relationship with God and with one another. First, we are told that now we know God. Through Jesus Christ, God has been made known to us. Charity counsels broad and nonpreferential love, but friendship adds to charity knowledge. In a divine-human encounter, that knowledge is profound. God loves us; God also knows who we are. Similarly, we know God. Through Jesus Christ God has given us knowledge of who God is and how God is.

Second, our knowledge of God through Jesus Christ decisively alters the character of our relationship to God. We know who and how God is. We no longer obey God because God says so. This is a slavery that has passed away with the incarnation. Rather, we obey

God because we know, in some ultimate way, what God is doing. Indeed, we know too much! It would be easier if we were slaves or servants, ignorant of the Master's purposes.

Third, our knowledge of God through Jesus Christ decisively alters the character of our sin before God. Disobedience is the sin in a master-slave relationship, but the sin in friendship is betrayal.

Finally, our knowledge of God through Jesus Christ confers on us a special kind of equality among those who share that knowledge. This is the powerful witness of Jesus' friendship with tax collectors and sinners. Jesus didn't simply give food to those who were hungry. He *ate* with them! In that gesture, he crossed the line between charity into friendship. This is the model of "power with" or friendship that Jesus proffers.

Images of Community

This image of God alerts us to the mutuality we have with God in God's kingdom and calls us to an active responsibility in working toward that kingdom. We are thus relieved of the passive obedience that a master-slave relationship would demand and that an understanding of coercive power would reinforce. We are equally eased away from the idolatry of creating our own kingdom in God's name, the possibility present in "power within." Images of God as Friend engender a community that is counseled to be loyal and cautioned against betrayal.

Moreover, images of God as Friend suggest by analogy that we be friends to one another. Beneath the solidarity among friends engaged in a common struggle is the God who commands us to love one another and who in God's self models the kind of coactive power that sustains that love. This spiritual friendship echoes the words of Aelred of Rievaulx, who prescribed for his brothers in community the kind of friendship that "begins in Christ, is preserved according to the Spirit of Christ, and its end and fruition are referred to Christ."[17]

Images of Leadership

A leader operating in this kind of "power with" mode would be living out of a calling to be "first among equals" *(primus inter pares)*. The task would be one of fidelity to a common good and active work toward that goal. Rather than being at the top of a pyramid of power, as in the "power over" model, or at the hub of a centrifuge, as in the "power within" model, the leader would be the head of the body, directing movement that he or she would not be able to complete on his or her own. An organic metaphor for community best describes the mutuality present in a community organized around friendship.

And yet, "power with" has its own problems, perhaps best illustrated in the caricatures of leader as Buddy or Terminal Facilitator. These caricatures surface when a group loses sight of its common purpose; all that remains is cloying intimacy or terminal process with no product apparent and no end in sight. As buddy, the leader is merely "one of the folks," close and amiable, but precisely for that proximity unable to empower, direct, or chasten any one of the group. As facilitator, a leader is good at getting out the possibilities that lie within the group. But mere facilitation neither challenges nor empowers the group to transcend itself and seek possibilities that lie beyond it. In general, the friendship model of leadership often constitutes a denial of differences in power between leader and group. It also denies responsibilities that rest—and rest only—with the leader. The caricatures of leader as Buddy and Terminal Facilitator point to real problems with "power with" leadership, and these must be held in tension with the equally real possibilities latent in the same model.

Drawing Things Together

Into the Kitchen!

At the beginning of his *Postmodern Geographies*, Edward Soja confronts the reader with a chapter entitled "Preface and Postscript." His introduction is his conclusion, and he wants above all to unfold his text as a map, rather than present it as a linear argument.[1] "The discipline imprinted in a sequentially unfolding narrative predisposes the reader to think historically, making it difficult to see the text as a map, a geography of simultaneous relations and meanings that are tied together by a spatial rather than a temporal logic."[2]

Soja hopes to defeat the linear flow of language in both speech and writing and to construct a "spatial logic" that makes visible relationships between various parts of his cognitive landscape and allows events to happen simultaneously.

If Soja is a cartographer and argues a "spatial logic," then I will follow M. F. Fisher, argue a gastronomic logic, and call for a feast. Preparation of any savory dish involves identifying the ingredients that are available and necessary, listing and purchasing materials, scrubbing, chopping, and sorting them. This is the analytical moment in cooking. A friend considers it the worst part of the enterprise, unworthy even of the name of "cooking." I prefer to see it as the first moment. This is undoubtedly why we like to cook together.

But as time marches on, the various ingredients, prepared, chopped, and sauteed, are brought together into a whole. This is the synthetic moment in cooking, and those who savor it also often love to extend it. The excellence of any dish is directly proportional to the amount of time involved in preparation.

Then, of course, there is the aesthetic moment, which culminates in the eating and which, to my mind, ought to last at least as long as the preparation.

The danger of every typology like this one is that the cook will complete the tasks of identifying, sorting, and chopping—and then either be too tired to continue or find that she is no longer hungry. The task of analysis will have become an end in itself, and everyone goes hungry. The synthetic and aesthetic moments will have been lost in the flurry of excessive preparation.

Acknowledging all of this, I confess that there is nothing I can do about any of it. The synthetic and aesthetic tasks rightly belong to the reader. Every reader will invariably see his image more sharply in one or the other of the types presented. But he will also see his image, if only myopically, in one of the other types as well. Perhaps he will even remember occasions on which he might more appropriately or more effectively or more faithfully have used one of the other forms of power. Indeed, the intent of such a typology is neither to argue for the excellence of one of the other models nor to argue for three mutually exclusive models of power. Rather, the intent of this typology is to suggest that the three models together exist in dynamic equilibrium and appear in each of our lives in delicate and unique proportions.

Revisiting the Case Studies

There are differences in degree and not in kind between the various case studies. Kevin, the music minister from the first case study, also has the strong markings of a charismatic leader. He is energetic, inspirational, and easily liked. In fact, it's quite possible that Kevin prefers to exercise his power as a charismatic figure, shunning the more institutional power that his colleague possesses and which has in fact been conferred on him as well. It is not that Kevin does not *have* institutional power in his position; it is the case that Kevin chooses not to exercise that power. This disdain for institutional power is common enough in young people, but the alternative is a personal, intimate leadership—which has its own problems. Kevin's final session with the adult choir degenerates into an exchange of personal attacks and *ad hominem* remarks.

At the same time, this first case study could also be used as a case study in coactive power, if only we knew more about the congregation! Clearly, Kevin had the support of parents whose youth came in ever-increasing numbers to the youth groups and the youth choir. Where were they in the final showdown? Where were the youth and the children in the midst of all this? Did anyone talk to them, the ones whose silence and whose absence are most glaring in the case study as presented? What were they told? What might they have said? Kevin also created a unique spirit in the adult choir, as they worked to master the intricacies of jazz harmony and rhythm. What happened to that spirit and that solidarity? Answers to these questions would entail far more information than the case study provides. Yet, it is also important to acknowledge the gaps, the silences, the words we do not have from people we do not know.

Similarly, the second case study, "The Pastor and the Church Matriarch," illumines particular facets of charismatic power. Yet, as was acknowledged in the analysis of that case, the church matriarch is not the only bearer of charismatic power. Indeed, the entire congregational dynamic could be analyzed as a transition from one female charismatic figure, Ruth, to another charismatic female figure, Pastor Jane. Not only is pastor Jane recognized as having a great deal of charismatic power, but the institution has legitimated it by calling her as pastor to the congregation. Unlike Ruth, Jane's power has been authorized; the charisma has been routinized.[3] This suggests a personal difference between the two women, but it also suggests a political difference. Separated in age by about twenty years, Jane has been able to move into ministry in a church that has only recently opened its ordained clergy to women. Ruth simply did not have that opportunity. Their conflict is more than merely a personal one; it is set up and sanctioned by institutions. One might well speculate whether many Protestant churches started ordaining women and integrating them into the bureaucracy of the institution, so that it would not have to deal with their charismatic leadership elsewhere!

At the same time, the case study could well be used to illustrate a kind of coactive power operative in the congregation, around and in spite of the conflict between two of its most formidable leaders. While Ruth and Pastor Jane are waging war on the battlegrounds of the words of the Bible and the bodies of Laotian immigrants, the congregation fills the vacuum of leadership itself. Members gather and prepare various departure celebrations for Ruth. They review a previous consensus on inclusive language and decide *not* to make a policy decision on the matter, but to leave the language of the Bible up to the individual lectors. The women decide that they really don't need a president for their group and continue leaderless. The conflict between these two powerful women would have been enough to make anyone shy about taking a position of authority! But there is strong evidence of coactive leadership at St. Paul's.

Finally, the last case study, "The Healers," was presented as an illustration of coactive leadership or friendship. Certainly, for the brief space of a summer a vision was created and implemented. Yet, when Mary returned, not quite a year later, the Thursday morning Healing Service and Eucharist was exactly as she had found it upon arrival the summer before: again in need of "new energy." But whose judgment was it that the service needed "new energy"? Had those rendering that judgment really noticed the energy that may have quietly been there all along? Is "energy" measured always by body count and in number and intensity of intimate, interpersonal contacts? Is this always the measure of success in a church? Where is there room for the faithful introvert, who wishes nothing more than a brief space of solace in which to contemplate the mysteries?

In view of the huge network of telephone trees, the schedules of pick-ups for transportation to and from the service, the calls cataloging who was ill and with what or who was grieving and why, the case study could well be an illustration of an emerging *corporatio sanctorum*, which toppled when its chief executive officer departed to go back to seminary. The entire summer could be evaluated as an example of burgeoning bureaucratic exercise of "power over."

Is there not some of the charismatic figure here as well? With her clear gifts for preaching and speaking, her willingness to listen, her creativity, Mary certainly qualifies. She sees the potential for a larger prayer ministry that might provide a spiritual foundation for the many programs in which members were involved. Everyone seems excited, and the vision catches fire. But why did the vision not persist after her departure? Was it actively resisted by the rectors, a possible intervention of sovereign or bureaucratic power? Was Mary's inspirational charismatic leadership strong enough or sustained over a sufficient amount of time for her vision to catch? Were her congregants really able and willing to work together? We have no answers to these questions, but each question opens up different dimensions of the case under study. At least these dimensions—and perhaps many more!—are present in the complex mix that is called congregational life.

With this observation, we confront both a weakness and a strength in typological thinking. The weakness is that typological thinking can encourage a kind of monofocal perspective on a situation. The story "The Music Minister and the Preacher" illustrates "power over"; the story "The Pastor and the Church Matriarch" illustrates "power within"; the story "The Healers" illustrates "power with." To the degree that I have used each story to illustrate a particular form of power, I have encouraged a kind of monofocal vision which may not be the whole picture—or even enough of the whole. But a strength of typological thinking is to create various points of vantage from which one can glimpse different dimensions of a specific situation.

Although the case study "The Music Minister and the Preacher" illustrates nicely "power over," to view it from the other perspectives of power opens up different aspects of the case. One is forced to consider the role of the congregation or the kind of charismatic leadership Kevin exercised.

Although the case study "The Pastor and the Church Matriarch" illustrates abstract discussion of charismatic power, when viewed from other perspectives new dimensions of the case emerge. One is forced to consider the coalescence of bureaucratic and charismatic power in the role of pastor, the changing role of women in the churches over the last few decades, or the role of the congregation in the struggle between Ruth and Pastor Jane.

Although the case study "The Healers" frames coactive power or friendship, when seen from these other points of vantage, the case challenges us to consider how quickly a grass roots movement can become bureaucratic, how hard it is to empower people through inspirational charismatic leadership, or the source of judgments like "This service needs more energy." A strength of typological thinking is in opening up various points of vantage on a difficult situation.

Another strength of typological thinking is in helping to clarify difficult situations in the first place. Even considering a situation like that presented in "The Music Minister and the Preacher" from the vantage point of "power over" moves the case from a personal conflict between Kevin and Robert to a nexus of more complex dynamics involving the entire congregation, the college, even the relationship between congregations and church adjudicatories. Considering the case study "The Pastor and the Church Matriarch" from the vantage point of "power within" moves the situation from a conflict between two powerful women to a study of the effects of charismatic leadership upon a group. Considering the case study "The Healers" from the vantage point of "power with" raises the question of local empowerment within the circumstances of a large congregation.

The clarity provided by a typological model is to see leadership as a complex mix of personal, communal, and institutional dynamics. It renders impossible—or at least naive!—a simple descriptive answer to the question, "What is your leadership style?" The leader being interrogated can only reply, "It depends."

Pressed to elaborate, the leader can only say: "It depends upon me, of course, but it also depends on who, where, and in what situation." Certainly, it depends on the leader, her particular strengths, weaknesses, and proclivities. But it also depends on the community and its peculiar dynamics and patterns of relating. Moreover, it depends on the institutions connected to both leader and community.

After all, the women's group, which Ruth had so long led, was a chapter in a larger organization to which Pastor Jane was the chaplain. Kevin was working in a church in which the board of deacons had a great deal of power, but which was also a body to which he had no direct accountability. Mary worked as a summer intern, with fixed arrival and departure dates. Despite her prior relationship to the congregation, she entered that summer as an outsider, with all the enthusiasm and vision only an outsider can have. But she also had a concrete termination. How did that affect both her vision and the way it was perceived? Structural concerns invade each of these cases in often unnoticed ways, when they are viewed from typological points of vantage.

Thinking Theologically About Power

I have suggested that the typological points of vantage introduce the structural and political dimensions of the case.

This particular typology has also introduced the theological dimensions of leadership. The exercise of "power over," whether in its sovereign, parental, or bureaucratic form, is informed and transformed by a divine power that pours itself out upon the whole of creation. At once we meet a God who is both other and gift. The encounter counsels humility and challenges tendencies of domination, parentilization, and bureaucratization in this form of power. What if Robert had called Kevin after the Christmas holidays were over and invited him to Sunday brunch, initiating conversation over a meal? What if Kevin had asked for an appointment with Robert, as he handed in his resignation? What if the board of deacons had requested an interview with both men?

The exercise of "power within," hypnotic and charismatic, is informed and transformed by a divine power that is the source of all spiritual gifts. At once we meet a God who is both in us and outside us, in constant motion, a God we can neither capture nor build a booth to shelter. The encounter counsels discernment for the presence of this God and challenges tendencies of idolatry and domination in this form of power. What if either Ruth or Pastor Jane had followed up immediately upon the conversation Pastor Jane suggested they needed to have? What if the congregation had invited Pastor Jane to Ruth's good-bye parties?

The exercise of "power with" is informed by a divine power that eats, drinks, and sleeps with "tax collectors and sinners." At once we meet a God who has been revealed as friend and advocate. The encounter challenges tendencies of elitism and exclusivism in this form of power. What if the people who'd been at the first Healing Service and Eucharist had been asked or invited to the generative meeting? They were, after all, the ones who felt the service had enough "energy" for them to continue coming. What if the rectors, who'd judged that the service needed "new energy," had been more involved in generating that energy?

Thinking theologically invites new perspectives into the complex mix that is congregational life. It invites us as leaders and as followers to be attentive to the movements of a triune God within our most common settings. It invites us to experience and to articulate where God is present and active in our quotidian world and how God is present and active: as other and as gift, as dynamic presence, and as friend.

Personal dynamics are certainly at stake! We need only to remember Kevin and Robert, Ruth and Pastor Jane, Mary and a generative group that wanted her to show them what to do. So also are structural and institutional dynamics present. Many churches have internal governing bodies and national judicatories to which they are closely or loosely related. Churches exist in communities to which they are called to minister. All churches seek to inspirit and initiate programs that feed people and minister to their needs. But there are also divine dynamics at work in any encounter, part of the network of powers in which we all circulate. Where are these divine dynamics bidding and directing?

The question has no answer without a specific situation. Nor should it. A God who is creative, dynamic, and incarnate will move through our lives in ways that are ever surprising, if only we are able to see.

This is always the challenge the Mermaid presents. Just when we think we have sorted out the terrestrial universe most creatively, we catch a faint whiff of salt air and feel a tug at the elbow. The cosmos we've created collapses with the rather daunting certainty that, indeed, we will need to learn how to swim.

Notes

Preface

1. From Lisel Mueller's poem "For a Thirteenth Birthday," in her book, *The Need to Hold Still* (Baton Rouge: Louisiana State University Press, 1980), pp. 3-4.

2. Michel Foucault, "Two Lectures," in Colin Gordon, ed., *Power/Knowledge: Selected Interviews and Other Writings, 1972-1977* (New York: Pantheon Books, 1980). "Power must be analysed as something which circulates, or rather as something which only functions in the form of a chain. It is never localised here or there, never in anybody's hands, never appropriated as a commodity or piece of wealth. Power is employed and exercised through a net-like organisation. And not only do individuals circulate between its threads; they are always in the position of simultaneously undergoing and exercising this power" (p. 98).

3. See, for example, Starhawk's *Truth or Dare: Encounters with Power, Authority, and Mystery* (San Francisco: Harper & Row, 1987), pp. 8-16.

4. See, for example, Hannah Arendt, *The Human Condition* (Chicago: University of Chicago Press, 1958); Rita Nakashima Brock, *Journeys by Heart: A Christology of Erotic Power* (New York: Crossroad, 1988); Anna Case-Winters, *God's Power: Traditional Understandings and Challenges* (Louisville: John Knox Press, 1990); Nancy Chodorow, *The Reproduction of Mothering* (Berkeley: University of California Press, 1978); Rebecca Chopp, *The Power to Speak: Feminism, Language, God* (New York: Crossroad, 1989); Nancy Hartsock, *Money, Sex, and Power: Toward a Feminist Historical Materialism* (Boston: Northeastern University Press, 1983); Karen Lebacqz, *Professional Ethics: Power and Paradox* (Nashville: Abingdon Press, 1985); Robin Tolmach Lakoff, *Talking Power: The Politics of Language* (New York: Basic Books, 1990); Adrienne Rich, *Of Women Born: Motherhood as Experience and Institution* (Boston: W. W. Norton, 1986); Starhawk, *Truth or Dare: Encounters with Power, Authority, and Mystery* (New York: Harper & Row, 1987); Haunani-Kay Trask, *Eros and Power: The Promise of Feminist Theory* (Philadelphia: University of Pennsylvania Press, 1986); Mariana Valverde, *Sex, Power and Pleasure* (Philadelphia: New Society Publishers, 1987).

Introduction

1. Robert Fulghum, *All I Really Need to Know I Learned in Kindergarten* (New York: Ivy Books, 1986), pp. 81-83.

2. See Sallie McFague's discussion of metaphor and parable in her *Metaphorical Theology: Models of God in Religious Language* (Philadelphia: Fortress Press, 1982), esp. pp. 32-54. McFague notes that "a theology influenced by parables would be open-ended, tensive, secular, indirect, iconoclastic, and revolutionary" (p. 48).

3. Cf. Steven Lukes, ed., *Power* (Oxford: Basil Blackwell, 1986); Steven Lukes, *Power: A Radical Analysis* (London: Macmillan, 1974); David Bell, *Power, Influence, and Authority* (New York: Oxford University Press, 1975); Peter Blau, *Exchange and Power in Social Life* (New York: Wiley, 1964); Brian Barry, ed., *Power and Political Theory: Some European Perspectives* (New York: Wiley, 1976); Hannah Arendt, *The Human Condition* (Chicago: University of Chicago Press, 1958); Hannah Arendt, *On Violence* (New York: Harcourt, Brace, and World, 1969); Dorothy Emmet, "The Concept of Power," *Proceedings of the Aristotelian Society* (London) n.s. 54 (1953–1954); Hanna Pitkin, *Wittgenstein and Justice* (Berkeley: University of California Press, 1972); Elizabeth Janeway, *Powers of the Weak* (New York: Alfred E. Knopf, 1980); Nancy Hartsock, *Money, Sex, and Power* (Boston: Northeastern University Press, 1983); Colin Gordon, ed., *Power/Knowledge: Selected Interviews and Other Writings, 1972–1977* (New York: Pantheon Books, 1980); Paul Rabinow, ed., *The Foucault Reader* (New York: Pantheon Books, 1984); Karen Lebacqz, *Professional Ethics: Power and Paradox* (Nashville: Abingdon Press, 1985).

4. Michel Foucault, "Two Lectures: Lecture Two, 14 January 1976," in Colin Gordon, ed., *Power/Knowledge: Selected Interviews and Other Writings, 1972–1977* (New York: Pantheon Books, 1980), p. 98.

5. The word "integrate" is chosen deliberately. "Integrate," like "include," suggests that something or someone is "let into" a larger whole, which considers itself given, unchanging, and immutable.

6. Karen Lebacqz, *Professional Ethics: Power and Paradox* (Nashville: Abingdon Press, 1985), p. 119.

7. For ecclesiastical statements, see: The Special Committee on Human Sexuality, "Presbyterians and Human Sexuality, 1991," Office of the General Assembly of the Presbyterian Church (U.S.A.), Louisville, 1991; Task Force on Human Sexuality, "Human Sexuality and Christian Faith," Division for Church and Society, Evangelical Lutheran Church in America, Chicago, 1991; *The Blue Book: Reports of the Committees, Commissions, Boards, and Agencies of the General Convention of the Episcopal Church*, Phoenix, Ariz., July 1991, pp. 197ff.

8. *The Christian Century* notes that sexuality, along with war and dissension, was one of the top religion stories in 1991. See the *Christian Century* 108:37 (December 18-25, 1991), pp. 1187-90.

9. Michel Foucault, "We 'Other' Victorians," in Paul Rabinow, ed., *The Foucault Reader* (New York: Pantheon Books, 1984), p. 299. Emphasis mine.

10. By "problematized" I mean literally "rendered a problem or an issue." Perhaps the best illustration is the response of a laywoman and lesbian, who was attending one of her church's open hearings on homosexuality. "This is no 'issue,' " she cried with no small frustration. "This is my *life!*"

11. *The Journal of Christopher Columbus*, trans. Cecil Jane (London: Hakluyt Society, 1960), p. 46.

12. Mary Louise Pratt, *Imperial Eyes: Travel Writing and Transculturation* (New York: Routledge, 1992), p. 33. Pratt goes on to discuss the similarities in naming between navigational mapping and the developing sciences of natural history.

13. Cf. Matthew 16:13-23; Mark 8:27-33; Luke 9:18-22.

14. On the development of the primacy of the bishop of Rome, see Geoffrey Barraclough, *The Medieval Papacy* (New York: W. W. Norton, 1968); Henry Chadwick, *The Early Church* (Middlesex, England: Penguin Books, 1967), esp. chap. 16; and Robert B. Eno, S. S., *The Rise of the Papacy* (Wilmington, Del.: Michael Glazier, Inc., 1990).

15. See the story of Perpetua and her maidservant, Felicitas, in Patricia Wilson-Kastner, G. Ronald Kastner, Ann Millin, Rosemary Rader, Jeremiah Reedy, eds., *A Lost Tradition: Women Writers of the Early Church* (New York: University Press of America, 1981), pp. 19-30. A confrontation between Perpetua and her pagan father is illuminating on the power of naming. " 'Father,' I said, 'do you see here, for example, this vase, or pitcher, or whatever it is?' 'I see it,' he said. 'Can it be named anything else than what it really is?', I asked, and he said, 'No.' 'So I also cannot be called anything else than what I am, a Christian' " (p. 20).

16. "The main question is to know where we are in order to establish where we must go and where we have come from. Displacement is not only a metaphor; it is also the precise description of our condition," writes Brazilian theologian Vitor Westhelle, in "Creation Motifs in the Search for a Vital Space: A Latin American Perspective," in Susan Brooks Thistlethwaite and Mary Potter Engel, eds., *Lift Every Voice: Constructing Christian Theologies from the Underside* (San Francisco: Harper & Row, 1990), p. 130.

17. Cf. E. Franklin Frazier and C. Eric Lincoln, *The Negro Church in America/The Black Church Since Frazier* (New York: Schocken Books, 1974), pp. 20-23. Other spirituals express this longing for space quite poignantly:

> I've got a mother in de heaven,
> Outshines de sun,
> I've got a father in de heaven,
> Outshines de sun,
> I've got a sister in de heaven,
> Outshines de sun,
> When we get to heaven, we will
> Outshine de sun,
> Way beyond de moon.

18. Yi-Fu Tuan, *Space and Place: The Perspective of Experience* (Minneapolis: University of Minnesota Press, 1977), pp. 6-7. For other works on the importance of space, see Edward T. Hall, *The Hidden Dimension* (New York: Anchor/Doubleday, 1982); Edward W. Soja, *Postmodern Geographies: The Reassertion of Space in Critical Social Theory* (New York: Verso, 1989); Henri Lefebvre, *The Production of Space* (Cambridge, Mass.: Basil Blackwell Ltd., 1991).

19. Foucault, "Questions on Geography," in Gordon, ed., *Power/Knowledge*, p. 70.

20. "Space is fundamental in any form of communal life; space is fundamental in any exercise of power." Foucault, "Space, Knowledge, and Power," in Rabinow, ed., *The Foucault Reader*, p. 253.

21. See Michel Foucault, *Discipline and Punish: The Birth of the Prison* (New York: Vintage/Random House, 1979).

22. "Power is employed and exercised through a net-like organisation. And not only do individuals circulate between its threads; they are always in the position of simultaneously undergoing and exercising this power. They are not only its inert or consenting target; they are always also the elements of its articulation. In other

words, individuals are the vehicles of power, not its points of application." Foucault, "Two Lectures: Lecture Two, 14 January 1976," p. 98.

23. Richard Sennett, *Authority* (New York: Vintage/Random House, 1980), pp. 3-4. Sennett identifies the two other bonds of society as fraternity and loyalty. He acknowledges that these "bonds" can be quite ambivalent. They can be bonds in the sense of bondage or constraints upon one's action. Yet, these bonds can also express our deepest longings. As such, they are necessary and unavoidable. The question to be put to them regards their quality and duration. Sennett admits the fragility of all emotional bonds, and he is particularly conscious of the fragility of authority over time. This introduces a painful complexity: "Authority is not a state of being but an event governed by the rhythm of growing and dying" (p. 167). At another point he states: "We have a principle by which to criticize society based not on abstract deduction about justice and right but on our intimate knowledge of time" (p. 196). For similar insight about the role of time in the exercise of dominative power, see Jean Baker Miller's *Toward a New Psychology of Women* (Boston: Beacon Press, 1976), pp. 3-12.

24. This is Sennett's felicitous expression (*Authority*, p. 4).

25. Hannah Arendt, *The Human Condition* (Chicago: University of Chicago Press, 1958), p. 244.

26. See "Gay minister supported," *The Christian Century* 109:64 (January 22, 1992); Jorge Aquino, "Gay Issues Kept Alive for Presbyterians," *The Christian Century* 109:64 (January 22, 1992); "Feud Over Lesbian Pastor," *The Christian Century* 109:296 (March 18-25, 1992).

27. Lebacqz, *Professional Ethics*, p. 146.

28. Arendt incisively distinguishes "power" from "strength," "force," "violence," and "coercion." Her understanding of a leader's power as *empowerment* by the community is elaborated in *On Violence* (New York: Harcourt, Brace & World, 1970), p. 44.

29. See Hannah Arendt's discussion of the isolation involved in tyranny in *The Human Condition*, pp. 202-3.

30. The exchange between Pilate and the crowd is unusual and compelling in Matthew's Gospel. Yet, in his concern for order and church structure, it is not surprising that the author of Matthew's Gospel would show so graphically and negatively the power of an unruly crowd.

31. Elias Canetti, *Crowds and Power* (New York: Farrar Straus & Giroux, 1962), p. 49. Canetti identifies this biblical exchange between Pilate and the crowd as an example of the collective killing characteristic of baiting crowds. "The crowd advances towards victim and execution in order to rid itself once and for all of its own deaths" (p. 49). Canetti identifies specific elements of the power of crowds: force, speed, secrecy, judgment/condemnation, and pardon/mercy (pp. 281-99).

32. See Mary Parker Follett's *Dynamic Administration* (London: London Management Publications Trust, Ltd., 1934), quoted in Dorothy Emmet's article, "The Concept of Power" (Presidential address to the Aristotelian Society), *Proceedings of the Aristotelian Society* (London) n.s. 54 (1953–1954). Emmet notes that "the book is much better than the title suggests."

33. Max Weber, "The Sociology of Charismatic Authority," in H. H. Gerth and C. Wright Mills, eds., *From Max Weber: Essays in Sociology* (New York: Oxford University Press, 1958), pp. 245-52.

34. See, for example, Mary E. Hunt, *Fierce Tenderness: A Feminist Theology of Friendship* (New York: Crossroad, 1991); Janice Raymond, *A Passion for Friends: Toward a Philosophy of Female Affection* (Boston: Beacon Press, 1986); Lillian Rubin, *Just Friends* (New York: Harper & Row, 1985); Starhawk, *Truth or Dare:*

Encounters with Power, Authority, and Mystery (San Francisco: Harper & Row, 1987), and esp. Eleanor Humes Haney's early article on friendship as foundational to feminist ethics, "What Is Feminist Ethics? A Proposal for Continuing Discussion," *Journal of Religious Ethics* 8:1 (1980): 115-24.

Power I

1. See N. Lee Orr, *The Church Music Handbook* (Nashville: Abingdon Press, 1991).

2. John Kenneth Galbraith, "Power and Organization," in Steven Lukes, ed., *Power* (Oxford: Basil Blackwell, 1986).

3. Among these discussions are the following: Walter H. Slack, *The Grim Science: The Struggle for Power* (Port Washington, New York: Kennikat, 1981); C. Wright Mills, *The Power Elite* (Oxford: Oxford University Press, 1956); Donald W. Harward, ed., *Power: Its Nature, Its Use, and Its Limits* (Boston: G. K. Hall & Co., 1979); Starhawk, *Truth or Dare: Encounters with Power, Authority, and Mystery* (San Francisco: Harper & Row, 1987); Elizabeth Janeway, *Powers of the Weak* (New York: Alfred A. Knopf, 1980); Elias Canetti, *Crowds and Power* (New York: Viking Press, 1966); Michael Lerner, *Surplus Powerlessness: The Psychodynamics of Everyday Life and the Psychology of Individual and Social Transformation* (Oakland, Calif.: Institute for Labor and Mental Health, 1986).

4. It is from Lord Acton that we have the grim pronouncement, "Power tends to corrupt and absolute power corrupts absolutely." From a letter to Bishop Mandell Creighton, 5 April 1887. Rollo May argues that *powerlessness* corrupts in his *Power and Innocence: A Search for the Sources of Violence* (Boston: W.W. Norton, 1972), p. 23. The insight is repeated by clinical psychologist Michael Lerner: "Powerlessness corrupts. Powerlessness corrupts in a very direct way: It changes, transforms, and distorts us. It makes us different from how we would otherwise want to be. We look at our world and our own behavior, and we tell ourselves that although we really aren't living the lives we want to live, there is nothing we can do about it. We are powerless." Michael Lerner, *Surplus Powerlessness*, p. 2.

5. "Be fruitful and multiply, and fill the earth and subdue it; and have dominion over the fish of the sea and over the birds of the air and over every living thing that moves upon the earth" (Gen. 1:28).

6. Again, language betrays us. Think of the terms "natural resources" and "raw materials," which suggest that the environment is entirely at the disposal of human invention and perhaps even in need of human refinement.

7. The stage is set by Augustine, who notes that a created "dominion" of husband over wife, or parent over child, has turned into "domination" after the Fall. See Augustine, *The City of God*, xiv, 4, in David Knowles (ed.), *Concerning the City of God Against the Pagans* (New York: Penguin Books, 1972), pp. 552-54. Cf. R. A. Marcus, *Saeculum: History and Society in the Theology of St. Augustine* (Cambridge: Cambridge University Press, 1970), pp. 198-99.

8. Nancy Hartsock, *Money, Sex, and Power: Toward a Feminist Historical Materialism* (Boston: Northeastern University Press, 1983), p. 2. Hartsock further urges an analysis of power as an important part of political philosophy: "A critique of theories that explain how power relations are constructed and how power is exercised can be an important resource for understanding what the construction of a more human community would require" (p. 2).

9. Starhawk, *Truth or Dare*, p. 9. In crafting a psychology and spirituality of

liberation, Starhawk presents a threefold typology: power-over, power-within, and power-with. She dismisses the first form of power entirely, focusing her attention on the second and third forms of power. Although I am indebted to her typology as a helpful heuristic device, I cannot follow all of her conclusions and assessments. These three forms of power *all* have their uses and abuses. Thus, I see the positive uses of power-over and abuses of both power-with and power-within, none of which Starhawk explores.

10. "Thus, the point of having power over another is to liberate the other rather than dominate or even kill her." Hartsock, *Money, Sex, and Power*, p. 257. Hartsock notes the conjunction of eros, power, and death, a conjunction replicated in the Library of Congress cataloguing system. Books on power, sexuality, and death are all within a few shelves and call numbers of each other.

11. Carter Heyward, *Touching Our Strength: The Erotic as Power and the Love of God* (San Francisco: Harper & Row, 1989), p. 35. See also Jean Baker Miller's *Toward a New Psychology of Women* (Boston: Beacon Press, 1986), pp. 3-12.

12. Michael Taussig, *Shamanism, Colonialism, and the Wild Man: A Study in Terror and Healing* (Chicago: University of Chicago Press, 1987), p. 446.

13. See esp. Karen Lebacqz and Ronald G. Barton, *Sex in the Parish* (Louisville: Westminster/John Knox Press, 1991); Marie M. Fortune, *Is Nothing Sacred: When Sex Invades the Pastoral Relationship* (San Francisco: Harper & Row, 1989); Peter Rutter, *Sex in the Forbidden Zone* (Los Angeles: Jeremy P. Tarcher, 1989).

14. Conversations with Pacific School of Religion professor of ethics Dr. Karen Lebacqz have clarified this point.

15. In the class in which this case study was presented, this particular case was one among several involving conflicts in power between pastors and organists, pastors and church musicians, worship leaders and choir directors. Finally, a student, wishing to address a conflict that involved neither music nor musicians, entitled her case study, "The Case of the Missing Church Organist"! Beneath the humor, however, was a serious statement about the subliminal power of both music and ritual in worship and the very tenuous authority of the people who are in charge of them.

16. See Herbert Musurillo's, *The Acts of the Christian Martyrs* (Oxford: Clarendon Press, 1972).

17. Musurillo, *Acts of the Christian Martyrs*, pp. 106-31. See also Rosemary Rader's translation and notes in Patricia Wilson-Kastner, G. Ronald Kastner, Ann Millin, Rosemary Rader, Jeremiah Reedy, *The Lost Tradition: Women Writers of the Early Church* (Lanham, New York: University Press of America, 1981), pp. 1-32. "As he fell on his face I stepped on his head. Then the people began to shout and my assistants started singing victory songs. I walked up to the trainer and accepted the branch. He kissed me and said, 'Peace be with you, my daughter.' And I triumphantly headed towards the Sanavivarian Gate" (pp. 24-25).

18. See the chapter entitled "The Erotic Dimension and the Homeric Ideal," in Hartsock, *Money, Sex, and Power*, pp. 186-204. In this chapter Hartsock analyzes and problematizes the warrior community. Although I accept her analysis, I question the problematization. It does not acknowledge that many communities which have resisted oppression have often spoken the language of the warrior and created communities of resistance. For this reason, I have chosen to juxtapose Hartsock's negative assessment of warrior communities alongside communities of early Christian martyrs, in order to illumine a more positive assessment of warrior communities.

19. In H. Richard Niebuhr's typology, these would be the "Christ against culture" model of churches. See his *Christ and Culture* (San Francisco: Harper & Row, 1951), pp. 45-82.

20. Hannah Arendt, *On Violence* (New York: Harcourt, Brace & World, 1970), p. 44. See also *The Human Condition* (Chicago: University Press, 1958), p. 200, where Arendt offers an eloquent restatement: "Power is actualized only where word and deed have not parted company, where words are not empty and deeds not brutal, where words are not used to veil intentions but to disclose realities, and deeds are not used to violate and destroy but to establish relations and create new realities." Richard Sennett has also commented on reciprocity, or "give-and-take," as he calls it, the "missing dimension" in modern approaches to authority. See his *Authority* (New York: Vintage/Random House, 1980), p. 25.

21. Arendt, *The Human Condition*, p. 202. Arendt continues: "Montesquieu realized that the outstanding characteristic of tyranny was that it rested on isolation—on the isolation of the tyrant from his subjects and the isolation of the subjects from each other through mutual fear and suspicion—and hence that tyranny was not one form of government among others but contradicted the essential human condition of plurality, the acting and speaking together, which is the condition of all forms of political organization. Tyranny prevents the development of power, not only in a particular segment of the public realm but in its entirety; it generates, in other words, impotence as naturally as other bodies politic generate power."

22. See, for example, Nel Nodding's *Caring: A Feminine Approach to Ethics and Moral Education* (Berkeley: University of California, 1984); Nancy Chodorow, *The Reproduction of Mothering: Psychoanalysis and the Sociology of Gender* (Berkeley: University of California Press, 1978); Jean Baker Miller, *Toward a New Psychology of Women* (Boston: Beacon Press, 1986); Sara Ruddick, *Maternal Thinking: Toward a Politics of Peace* (New York: Ballantine Books, 1990); Carol Gilligan, *In a Different Voice: Psychological Theory and Women's Development* (Cambridge, Mass.: Harvard University Press, 1982).

23. For critics of such an elevation of motherhood and its coordinate emphasis on caring and nurture, see Nancy Scheper-Hughes, *Death Without Weeping: The Violence of Everyday Life in Brazil* (Berkeley: University of California Press, 1992); Adrienne Rich, *Of Woman Born: Motherhood as Experience and Institution* (Boston: W. W. Norton, 1986).

24. These are embedded in the following works, although the synthesis is mine. See Heyward, *Touching Our Strength*, pp. 34-35; and Miller, *Toward a New Psychology of Women*, pp. 3-12.

25. Carter Heyward makes this point well: "Mutuality does not necessarily imply equality, nor does equality assure mutuality. Equality denotes a sameness of position or status, while mutuality describes a dynamic relational movement into a vision of ourselves together" (*Touching Our Strength*, p. 34).

26. Again, Carter Heyward is emphatic: "Any unequal power relationship is intrinsically abusive if it does not contain seeds both of transformation into a fully mutual relationship and of mutual openness to equality" (*Touching Our Strength*, p. 35). But see also Miller's discussion, *Toward a New Psychology of Women*, pp. 3-12.

27. Paul Rabinow observes that Michel Foucault saw Jeremy Bentham's plan for the panopticon as a paradigm of disciplinary technology. Rabinow describes the coalition of space, power, control of the body, and control of groups that makes this possible. "The panopticon consists of a large courtyard, with a tower in the center, surrounded by a series of buildings divided into levels and cells. In each cell there are two windows: one brings in light and the other faces the tower, where large observatory windows allow for the surveillance of the cells. The cells become 'small theatres, in which each actor is alone, perfectly individualized and constantly visible.' The inmate is not simply visible to the supervisor; he is visible to the supervisor alone—cut off from any contact. This new power is continuous and

anonymous." "Introduction," *The Foucault Reader* (New York: Pantheon Books, 1984), p. 19.

28. Richard Sennett, *Authority*, p. 22. Sennett identifies this definition as the Weberian legacy on the subject. To this, he juxtaposes the Freudian perspective on authority: authority as "the process by which people perceive strength in others, apart from the content of what they perceive" (p. 22). Neither approach, he writes, takes into account "the actual give-and-take between the strong and the weak . . . how an interpretation is constructed through social exchange" (pp. 25-26). Sennett proposes to address what he feels to be the crisis of authority in our time: "We feel attracted to strong figures we do not believe to be legitimate" (p. 26).

29. Sennett, *Authority*, pp. 179-86. In team-teaching a course on power and eros, my colleague, Clare B. Fischer, professor at Starr King School of Ministry in Berkeley, California, and I experimented with three kinds of syllabuses. Our first used a passive voice, which masked *who* was doing the requiring ("Final papers will be required . . ."). Our second employed active voice, but masked the subjects through use of third-person plural ("The instructors require . . ."). Our final syllabus took the form of a letter, using active voice and first-person plural ("We want . . ."). In the transition from the first to the third syllabuses, we found that we simply could not say the same kinds of things and say them in the same way in the final syllabus as we had in the first. For example, we had to move from legislative language ("Final papers will be *required* . . ." and "The instructors *encourage* you to . . ." and "We *want* . . .").

30. See Martha Ellen Stortz, "The Inscrutability of God and the Possibility of Political Community: Augustine's Political Theology," in *Halcyon: A Journal of the Humanities* 10 (1988): esp. 106-7.

Power II

1. For further reference, see Hans von Campenhausen, *Ecclesiastical Authority and Spiritual Power in the Church of the First Three Centuries* (Stanford: Stanford University Press, 1969). Bengt Holmberg, *Paul and Power: The Structure of Authority in the Primitive Church as Reflected in the Pauline Epistles* (Philadelphia: Fortress Press, 1980); John Howard Schutz, *Paul and the Anatomy of Apostolic Authority* (Cambridge: Cambridge University Press, 1975). Philip Rousseau, *Ascetics, Authority, and the Church in the Age of Jerome and Cassian* (Oxford: Oxford University Press, 1978). Malherbe, et al.

2. Thomas Muentzer's words are fiery and filled with allusions to the Spirit. He spurned the Word of God in Scripture for the "true living Word of God." Elsewhere in "The Prague Manifesto" (1521), he proclaims himself one of the Elect of God: "I, Thomas Muentzer of Stolberg, confess before the whole Church and the whole world, wherever this letter may be displayed, that I can bear witness, with Christ and all the elect who have known me from my youth up, that I have used my utmost diligence, above all other men, that I might have or attain a higher understanding of holy invincible Christian Faith. Yet all the days of my life (God knows, I lie not) I have never been able to get out of any monk or parson the true use of faith, about the profitableness of temptation which prepares for faith in the Spirit of the Fear of the Lord, together with the condition that each elect must have in the Sevenfold Holy Ghost." "The Prague Manifesto" in Lowell H. Zuck, ed., *Christianity and Revolution: Radical Christian Testimonies, 1520–1650* (Philadelphia: Temple University Press, 1975), pp. 32-33.

3. Teresa of Avila recounts an interview with her confessor regarding a vision she had. She reports that she "saw" Christ beside her, and her confessor responds: "In

what form did you see him?" She replies that she did not "see" him in a visual sense. He asks: "How did you know it was he?" She tries to explain further, but meets only with more questions. Biographer Stephen Clissold tells the end of this conversation, reported by a witness. Shortly afterward, the confessor himself has a vision and reports to Teresa that he has "seen" Christ. She replies with mock horror, "Do not believe it, Father! Christ appeared to your Reverence? It could not have been Christ! Just think again!" See Stephen Clissold's *St. Teresa of Avila* (New York: Seabury Press, 1982), pp. 53-55. For Teresa's account, see her autobiography, E. Allison Peers, ed., *The Life of Teresa of Jesus: The Autobiography of St. Teresa of Avila* (New York: Image/Doubleday, 1960), pp. 248-52.

4. "Charisma, as a creative power, recedes in the face of domination, which hardens into lasting institutions, and becomes efficacious only in short-lived mass emotions of incalculable effects, as on elections and similar occasions. . . . We must now return to the economic factors, already mentioned above, which predominantly determine the routinization of charisma: the need of social strata, privileged through existing political, social, and economic orders, to have their social and economic positions 'legitimized.' They wish to see their positions transformed from purely factual power relations into a cosmos of acquired rights, and to know that they are thus sanctified. These interests comprise by far the strongest motive for the conservation of charismatic elements of an objectified nature within the structure of domination. Genuine charisma is absolutely opposed to this objectified form. It does not appeal to an enacted or traditional order, nor does it base its claims upon acquired rights. Genuine charisma rests upon the legitimation of personal heroism or personal revelation. Yet precisely this quality of charisma as an extraordinary, supernatural, divine power transforms it, after its routinization, into a suitable source for the legitimate acquisition of sovereign power by the successors of the charismatic hero. Routinized charisma thus continues to work in favor of all those whose power and possession is guaranteed by that sovereign power, and who thus depend upon the continued existence of such power." Max Weber, "The Meaning of Discipline," in H. H. Gerth and C. Wright Mills, eds., *From Max Weber: Essays in Sociology* (New York: Oxford University Press, 1958), p. 262.

5. Michael Taussig, *Shamanism, Colonialism, and the White Man: A Study in Terror and Healing* (Chicago: University of Chicago Press, 1987).

6. Dorothy Emmet, *Function, Purpose, and Powers: Some Concepts in the Study of Individuals and Societies* (Philadelphia: Temple University Press, 1972), p. 224. Emmet's discussion on ancient understandings of charismatic power is fascinating and deserves careful study. See her chapters on "Charismatic Power" and "Vocation," pp. 206-69.

7. Hannah Pitkin elaborates this notion of power as capacity or "power to" in her book, *Wittgenstein and Justice* (Berkeley: University of California Press, 1972), pp. 275-77.

8. Max Weber, "The Sociology of Charismatic Authority," in Gerth and Mills, eds., *From Max Weber*, pp. 245-52.

9. Ibid., p. 248.

10. Raymond Trevor Bradley, *Charisma and Social Structure* (New York: Paragon House, 1987), p. 42.

11. Yet, perhaps Weber was also correct about the need to "routinize" or institutionalize charisma, so that it is removed as a possibility for others. A street that moves from Berkeley into Oakland is named after Martin Luther King; high schools are named for him. Mother Teresa won the Nobel Prize for Peace in 1979. A university in El Salvador is named for Oscar Romero. Teresa of Avila was canonized. All charismatic power that is not demonized seems to be institutionalized.

12. Emmet, *Function, Purpose, and Powers*, pp. 233-34. Emmet's challenge is

even personal: "I cannot help thinking there is something rather Teutonic, suggesting the *Fuehrer-Prinzip*, about this description" (p. 233).

13. Cf. Jean Baker Miller, *Toward a New Psychology of Women* (Boston: Beacon Press, 1986), pp. 3-12.

14. "But Weber does not see that this individual flair, by which some people can raise the morale of others, is quite different from the desire of the leader to exact blind devoted obedience; yet without self-knowledge, and indeed a sense of humour on the part of the charismatist, there is always a danger that it may turn into this" (p. 236). "There can then be the humility and generosity of a person who acquires *mana* from being a creative sort of person" (p. 238). Emmet, *Function, Purpose, and Powers*.

15. "*Hybris* is not just ordinary boastfulness: it is the corruption due to pride and excessive confidence which is the special temptation of great men; and to the Greeks, it is the irreligious attitude *par excellence.*" Emmet, *Function, Purpose, and Powers*, p. 236.

16. Umberto Eco, *The Name of the Rose* (New York: Harcourt Brace Jovanovich, 1983).

17. See H. Richard Niebuhr, "The Doctrine of the Trinity and the Unity of the Church," *Theology Today* 3 (October 1946): 371-84.

18. "First, theories of power are implicitly theories of community. To examine these theories of power is to involve oneself in the questions of how communities have been constructed, how they have been legitimized, and how they might be structured in more liberatory ways." Nancy Hartsock, *Money, Sex, and Power: Toward a Feminist Historical Materialism* (Boston: Northeastern University Press, 1983), p. 3. Though Hartsock does not make this point, the reverse could also be true: Every theory of community is implicitly a theory of power. The response of feminists and blacks to *Habits of the Heart* and *The Good Society* was a sharp reminder that the theories of community elaborated in these books presumed power relations in terms of race, class, and gender that they found offensive. (See Cornel West's review in the *New York Times Book Review* 96:13 (Sept. 15, 1991).

19. For a fuller description of various images of God and the kinds of Christian community they delineate, see James M. Gustafson, *Can Ethics Be Christian?* (Chicago: University of Chicago Press, 1977), chap. 4.

Power III

1. Michael Taussig, *Shamanism, Colonialism, and the Wild Man: A Study in Terror and Healing* (Chicago: University of Chicago Press, 1987), p. 446.

2. Cited in Dorothy Emmet, "The Concept of Power," *Proceedings of the Aristotelian Society* n.s. 54 (1953–1954), p. 9, n. 7. See Mary Parker Follett's *Dynamic Administration* (London: London Management Publications Trust, 1934), p. 134. Follett juxtaposes "coercive power" with "coactive power," or "power over" with "power with." Note also Emmet's comment: "The book is much better than the title suggests."

3. Cf. Matthew 18:1-5; Mark 9:2-8; Luke 9:46-48 (a reference to the sons of Zebedee?).

4. Anthony C. Meisel and M. L. del Mastro, eds., *The Rule of St. Benedict* (New York: Image/Doubleday, 1974), p. 106.

5. Ibid., p. 47. See also Brian Patrick McGuire, *Friendship and Community: The Monastic Experience, 350–1250* (Kalamazoo, Mich.: Cistercian Publications, 1988).

6. Janice Raymond, *A Passion for Friends* (Boston: Beacon Press, 1986), p. 8. Raymond is not alone in turning to friendship for a constructive articulation of sisterhood. See Eleanor Humes Haney's early essay on friendship, "What Is Feminist

Ethics? A Proposal for Continuing Discussion," *Journal of Religious Ethics* 8/1 (1980): 115-24. Other books and essays have addressed the subject of "power with" or friendship: Mary E. Hunt, "Lovingly Lesbian: Toward a Feminist Theology of Friendship," in Robert Nugent, ed., *A Challenge to Love: Gay and Lesbian Catholics in the Church* (New York: Crossroad, 1983), and her latest book, *Fierce Tenderness: A Feminist Theology of Friendship* (New York: Crossroad, 1991); Lillian Rubin, *Just Friends: The Role of Friendship in Our Lives* (San Francisco: Harper & Row, 1985).

7. C. S. Lewis, *The Four Loves* (New York: Harcourt Brace Jovanovich, 1960), p. 122.

8. Nancy Hartsock, *Money, Sex, and Power: Toward a Feminist Historical Materialism* (Boston: Northeastern University Press, 1983), p. 2. Hartsock goes on to say, "There is, after all, a certain dangerous irony in the fact that both feminists and antifeminists agree that the exercise of power is a masculine activity and preoccupation, inappropriate to women or feminists, and not a subject to which attention should be directed" (p. 2).

9. The references are to key texts in the history of thinking about friendship: Plato's *Lysis*, Aristotle's *Nicomachean Ethics*, Cicero's *Laelius de amicitia*, and Aelred of Rievaulx's *Spiritual Friendship*. For a fascinating survey on theories of friendship in the classical world, see Horst Hutter, *Politics as Friendship: The Origins of Classical Notions of Politics in the Theory and Practice of Friendship* (Waterloo, Ontario, Canada: Wilfrid Laurier University Press, 1978). For an equally engaging survey of medieval texts and practices of friendship, see McGuire's *Friendship and Community*.

10. Raymond, *A Passion for Friends*, p. 29.

11. See Parker Palmer, *The Company of Strangers: Christians and the Renewal of America's Public Life* (New York: Crossroad, 1981).

12. Aristotle, *Nicomachean Ethics* 8.2-3. 1155a20 (New York: Bobbs-Merrill Co., Inc., 1962), p. 215.

13. Robert Bellah, et al., *Habits of the Heart* (Berkeley: University of California Press, 1985), p. 115. See also their later book, *The Good Society* (New York: Alfred A. Knopf, 1991).

14. Aristotle, NE. 8.7.1158b10-15, p. 227.

15. Aquinas, *ST* 22ae, Q.23.1.

16. See Thomas Flynn, "Foucault as Parrhesiast," in James Bernauer and David Rasmussen, eds., *The Final Foucault* (Cambridge: MIT Press, 1987).

17. Aelred of Rievaulx, *Spiritual Friendship* 1, 9 (Washington, D.C.: Cistercian Publications, 1974).

Drawing Things Together

1. My title, "Drawing Things Together," is also the title of an article by Bruno Latour, in Michael Lynch and Steve Woolgar, eds., *Representations in Scientific Practice* (Cambridge, Mass.: MIT Press, 1990). After analyzing the power of writing and inscription to "dominate all things and all people," Latour closes his essay: "If you want to understand what draws *things* together, then look at what *draws* things together" (p. 60).

2. Edward W. Soja, *Postmodern Geographies: The Reassertion of Space in Critical Social Theory* (New York: Verso, 1989), p. 1.

3. See Max Weber's discussion of genuine and routinized charisma in his essay, "The Meaning of Discipline," in H. H. Gerth and C. Wright Mills, eds., *From Max Weber: Essays in Sociology* (New York: Oxford University Press, 1958), pp. 262ff.

Index

253
ST886

LINCOLN CHRISTIAN COLLEGE AND SEMINARY 89001

253 ST886   89001
Stortz, Martha Ellen, 1952-
Pastorpower

DEMCO